About Bears We've Met

"From my crouched position I quickly looked in the direction of the noise to see three frightened brown bear cubs reeling backward from no more than ten feet behind me. What brought their roll to a halt would have my life flash before me in the intense moments to follow."

Come along with experienced naturalist and writer Joel Zachry, as he takes you to remote regions of North America where both black and brown bears abound. See through his eyes the mystery and wonder of these amazing animals as they have intrigued him throughout much of his life. Venture into habitats of breath-taking landscape and diversity of life, worthy of respect and preservation.

"With every cycle, she inhaled and exhaled in a low, guttural rattle. While I do not recall even a hint of her scent, as is often said to be observed in some encounters, I noted that even her dark lips had a wet, saliva-laden, glossy glow. We were that close."

Whether you are one of the participants that Joel and his wife Kathy have taken into the depths of the Great Smokies; led to Alaska in pursuit of the Last Frontier; or you are new to their adventures, you will delight in their encounters with bears as recalled herein.

"Just as surprised as we were, the black figure centered in the berry patch jerked upright and seemed to stare through us with intense dark eyes. There was little doubt what would happen next."

If we are truly to advance as a species, we must humble ourselves to recognize the importance and intrinsic value of wildlife as a major component of the Creation.

— Joel G. Zachry, M.S.

Bears We've Met

Short Stories of Close Encounters

JOEL G. ZACHRY WITH KATHY W. ZACHRY

authorHOUSE®

AuthorHouse™
1663 Liberty Drive
Bloomington, IN 47403
www.authorhouse.com
Phone: 1-800-839-8640

Great Outdoors! Adventure Travel
104 Zachry Drive
Kingston, TN 37763-7007

info@gowithgoat.com
www.gowithgoat.com

First published by AuthorHouse 5/04/2010

ISBN: 978-1-4520-0820-2 (sc)
ISBN: 978-1-4520-0821-9 (dj)

Photo credits: Joel and Kathy Zachry
About the Author photo credit: Dan Holcomb

Printed in the United States of America
Bloomington, Indiana

This book is printed on acid-free paper.

Dedication

I dedicate this book to all of our colleagues, friends, guests, participants, and students who have hiked and traveled with us over the years. Our lives are richer for the times we have spent with you among living things in these special places.

In Memory

Tommy Bennett

Friend, Companion, Nature Whiz

Don DeFoe

Exemplary Park Ranger, Friend, Gentleman

John Patten

Distinguished Professor, Mentor, Friend

Acknowledgments

*In my career at the college and university level, I was
very fortunate to have supervisors who believed in me,
encouraged my outdoor pursuits, and always lifted up me
up—I am grateful to Gayle Cooper, Mary Jerger, Anne
Minter, and Jim Kelley.*

I appreciate the support given my outdoor efforts by the
**National Park Service
Great Smoky Mountains National Park,**
*especially Glenn Cardwell, Ronnie Click, Babette Collavo,
Kim Delozier, Charles (Chuck) Hester, Debbie Huskey,
Gary Kuban, Bill Stiver, and "700."*

**Professional and Personal Development
The University of Tennessee,**
*especially Norvel Burkett, Marlene Burns, Linda Kallstrom,
Marjorie Lawson, and Nancy Orrick.*

Special recognition goes to all of the volunteers and staff of
Great Bear Foundation
*Matt Reid, I thank you for placing me in the midst of some
of the greatest bear advocates of our time—Barrie Gilbert,
Charles (Chuck) Jonkel, Lynn Rogers, and Charlie Russell.*

Appalachian Bear Rescue

Tom and Joni Caldwell, you were there for ABR
when the organization needed you the most.

Also, Robert (Bob) Myers, friend and mentor,
I could always depend upon you to attract a bear.

Most of all I honor you, Kathy my love, for you always
stood firm no matter what nature hurled at us.
You never faltered.

Preface

BOOKS ABOUT BEARS ARE NOTHING
NEW TO THE LITERARY WORLD.

For nearly two-thirds of my life, I have taught outdoor skills courses and led backcountry trips. During most of that time, Kathy, my wife, has been a faithful companion and equal contributor.

Throughout these years, I have been encouraged, by those who knew my passion for nature and writing, to record what we have learned from our experiences. Bears have taught us much.

I have always held a love for writing, and again those who know me know that I often express my deepest convictions in writing.

At the age of eighteen, as a college biology major, I wrote my first published piece on nature for our state conservation magazine, *The Tennessee Conservationist.* From that point forth, I have been eager to share my observations on the natural world with others.

In my career as a biologist, I became fascinated with bears as one of our Creator's best works. Interestingly, I never saw a bear (outside of a zoo and was never privy to many zoos growing up) until adulthood.

As my interest, knowledge, and experiences with them increased, I found that bear publications generally fell into one of three categories:

First, there were the "life history" publications depicting a bear's maturation from birth into adulthood with lifecycle pictures and descriptive captions, but little more.

Second, there were the scary manuscripts in which bear behavior at its worst was the central theme.

Third, there were research publications documenting years of data collected on bears.

Therefore, the point of this work is to fill a void by presenting short stories of close encounters that Kathy and I have experienced. In retrospect, several encounters were foolish blunders on our part; a few were very serious at the time they occurred, make no mistake; and our earlier responses to some encounters were quite humorous.

Most of the outdoor educational trips that we have led together have been in bear habitat. I never expected that she and I would encounter as many bears as we have experienced over the many years.

Sadly, for most of us the tales we learned in childhood depicted these intriguing animals as ferocious and harmful when in fact, they are generally a forgiving lot, if we only reciprocate and respect their need for space. Nonetheless, many wild animals have the potential to harm us with their defense mechanisms and we should *always* observe them with that in mind.

In this work I share some remarkable places that we came to know through our adventures together, each with their own intricate beauty and fascinating inhabitants. Spending time in these places with the creatures who live there has not only made our individual lives richer and more rewarding, but the trials of exploring these areas together have strengthened our relationship with each other.

Through this effort, I also want to stir a desire within the reader to go outdoors and enjoy these special places as we have—Alaska, the Appalachian Trail, Joyce Kilmer, Shenandoah, the Smokies, Yellowstone, and points beyond.

I want to educate the reader about bears as we have seen them and understood their behavior through our experiences, for they are animals worthy of our concern and care.

I hope that the reader will become more cognizant of the urgent need to preserve wild places and their stunning inhabitants. Our problems worldwide hinge on human population management. We must embrace that fact and act on it, else not only bears, but all will be lost.

Much of our population identifies only with those animals that easily adapt to life near humans, such as various songbirds and small game. Many fail to realize that when we continually expand our range, habitat for wildlife is altered, reduced, or eliminated altogether, and the loss of species diversity follows. Not only are numerous species destroyed, but others remain with no safe place to find shelter and food and live out their lives as their Creator intended.

For many people, state and national forests and parks offer infrequent observations of wildlife on annual vacation trips at best. It is not difficult to understand the lack of attention individuals give to wildlife issues and preservation efforts throughout much of the nation.

Bears are to the ecologist a "landscape species." If we allow them enough space plus resources for shelter, food, and water, then other, simpler life forms can also thrive. Bears are the ultimate symbols of wilderness, and thus provide a litmus test for a land's sustainability for other species.

Bears illustrate the marvel of birth and its journey toward death; the dependence of all creatures on each other; survival of the fittest; and all as it was designed to be.

So, read of bears here, then explore their mountains, forests, and woodlands and seek out what makes them unique. But do it softly and with respect for their habitat and reverence for their majesty.

Do everything you can to conserve, recycle, and speak out in support of nature and its intrinsic value to all of us. Avoid harm to any living creature, but know that each has its place and a right to live out its life here in its time.

Finally, it is said that God made wolves and man made dogs, so waste no energy attempting to improve wild things. Regard them as the special beings they are; enjoy the wonders of them; and cherish the value they add to our own lives the brief time we are here.

Joel G. Zachry, M.S.

Contents

Introduction

Kathy and I often are asked, "What is your favorite place to hike?"

There is no single one, for they are all special to us and each place is unique. How could one compare the Rockies to the Southern Appalachians and favor one over the other?

The Western mountains are higher, more exposed, rugged, and majestic. Trees are sparse, and the air is crisp and pure, giving way to cobalt skies where suddenly lightning bolts might appear and dance for miles across open spaces. In July and August, there is no greater beauty than a high alpine meadow carpeted in a multitude of colors, its wildflowers mere centimeters tall.

Winter sends most every furry creature scampering for hibernation, and snows blanket the landscape for months on end. The cold is penetrating as the ice thickens and the sounds of nature become mostly silent as it enjoys a long nap.

The Rockies have an abundance of stately and robust large mammals, too—bison, black and grizzly bear, mule and white-tailed deer, elk, moose, mountain lion, and pronghorn. The bears become lethargic and disappear into dens, while members of the cat and deer families struggle to remain predators and prey.

The older Eastern mountains do not compare in height but put up a strong fight for best of show with spring's bloodroot, trillium, spring beauty, trout lilies, and summer's heath blossoms. Vegetation is lush and thick, giving up moisture on humid days and sultry nights. A greater variety of flora is found here than in all of Europe.

Winters are mild, but higher elevations can compare in severity to those of the West. More temperate weather in the lowlands allows fauna to remain active, small game still abounds, and birdlife flourishes.

Alaska, the Last Frontier, fulfills the promise of what we all read about as kids but few experience its vastness and diversity as adults. We have been conducting small group backcountry trips there for twenty years, and there is no bad way to take in Alaska. It is all good—the people, the culture, its glaciers without end; the thousands of square miles with no cell towers, golf courses, or developments; and its seafood without rival.

So, whether we travel out West, along the Appalachian Trail, to the Last Frontier, or over the mountains on the Cherohala, bears dwell there, and they should! They are at the top of the food chain. Their ability to garner respect and space is the ultimate test of our humility. The presence of bears completes wilderness, and for many of us adds zest to exploration.

I believe that every living thing has a purpose and is vital to the existence of the next one. I do not squash ants on a picnic table, nor do I step on spiders in a parking lot, for given all of man's accolades—he has cured disease, stood on the moon, tantalized our palates with chocolate, opened the world to knowledge with the computer, and split the atom—he has yet to create a single gnat with wings so tiny they defy our eyes' ability to focus.

If the world survives another hundred years, the departure of the bear from our midst or its acceptance among us will define our advancement as a species. If we continue down the path of unwinnable arguments about global warming and cultural differences that divide us, all will perish along with the bear.

We can learn from bears. They spend time with their young teaching them how to exist in their world. They take only from their surroundings what they need to survive, and they coexist with other creatures, keeping life in balance.

I remember more than once Chuck Jonkel saying that the bruin views us as "a two-legged bear." Which will prove to be the wiser?

CHAPTER 1

Solar Eclipse

It was a sound that I would never forget.

*From my crouched position, I quickly looked in the direction
of the noise to see three frightened brown bear cubs reeling
backward from no more than ten feet behind me. What
brought their roll to a halt would have my life flash before
me in the intense moments to follow.*

It was August 1995, and this was my second trip to Kodiak Island, Alaska, as board member and officer of the Great Bear Foundation, a non-profit bear conservation organization headquartered at the time in Bozeman, Montana.

I had initially joined this organization by sending in my membership dues in 1992. After participating in a small group GBF excursion to Yellowstone National Park in May 1993, I became more convinced by their worthwhile mission to promote bear conservation issues. That November, I was voted onto the board of directors and later appointed board secretary and then president.

Being a part of this Montana-based group of not just bear enthusiasts but some of the greatest bear authorities, such as Dr. Barry Gilbert, Dr. Charles (Chuck) Jonkel, Dr. Lynn Rogers, and Charles (Charlie) Russell, was awe-inspiring. The energy and passion that Chuck Jonkel alone held for the bear was beyond my grasp at this point.

As someone who had grown up on a small East Tennessee hobby farm in the 1960s, there was so much to be said of traveling, not only to Alaska, but also to Kodiak Island. Finding me in Alaska was a major step out of the box from my rural upbringing, to say the least. To spend parts of two successive summers on the Emerald Isle, as it is known, in the presence of some of the world's most sizeable beings was unimaginable.

An archipelago is a chain of islands, and the Kodiak Archipelago is comprised of scattered land masses 250 miles southwest of Anchorage. It is only approachable by air or sea, and it encompasses more than 5,000 square miles, of which Kodiak Island is 3,588 of those miles. The majority of land on Kodiak falls within the Kodiak Wildlife Refuge, and its western Karluk Lake region is where we would spend our time.

The Island has fewer than 14,000 human residents and is home to more than 3,000 Kodiak brown bears, the largest land carnivores in North America. This equates to approximately one bear for every four residents of the island.

Interestingly, there have been few suspected human fatalities caused by the island's brown bears. I believe that this is because the locals and those who arrive to fish and hunt are somewhat knowledgeable in the ways of the bear and give them a wide berth.

My bear-viewing party included Matt Reid, GBF Executive Director; John Merrick, Land and Resource Manager for Koniag, Inc.; Steve Gehman, biologist and GBF associate; and Scott Shelton, our guide.

Matt and I had first traveled to Kodiak Island in the later part of May. I arrived in the town of Kodiak and flew in the front right-hand seat of a five-seat single engine plane whose pilot seemed to be no more than fifteen years of age. We journeyed less than an hour southeast and landed outside the village of Old Harbor, where Matt met the plane.

I can recall wondering if I would have trouble locating Matt in the airport but was surprised to learn that a meager landing strip was all there was. Additionally, we were clearly in the minority among the darker-skinned Alaskan natives with whom we would visit, dine, and stay for several days to come.

I had met Steve Gehman for the first time in 1993, and I became fond of him and respectful of his knowledge of nature during our Yellowstone trip together. He was easy to pick out in a crowd of other "bear people," for he handsomely sported bright red hair and flowing beard. He was not as chatty as Matt, and when he spoke there was reason to suspect that it was from a strong knowledge base and years of backcountry experience.

I liked Scott Shelton from the first meeting on Kodiak in May, when we stayed on Camp Island and were treated to his cooking and expertise on the Thumb River bears. He had a casual approach toward the bears, but he was serious when it came to protocol and avoiding potentially harmful encounters. He had a high respect for the power and natural instinct of the Kodiak bear, and rightfully so, for *he was living among them.*

John Merrick was obviously knowledgeable of the ways and affairs of the Kodiak natives. He seemed to take his position seriously, and I was confident that he was honorable in his dealings with the local people on land and bear issues.

This was late summer, and we were to spend the day observing brown bears who were feeding on migrating salmon as they moved about in the shallow Thumb River just below us. The pristine waters of the Thumb made their way swiftly beneath our perch and emptied fish, who were fortunate enough to escape awaiting bear paws, into Karluk Lake.

We would tally as many as forty-two bear sightings in one day as they ravaged their feeding grounds. A "sighting" meant a bear was seen, but it could represent a repeated observation of the same individual, unless there were specific markings that distinguished it from others. This manner of documenting what we saw avoided an exaggerated record of individual bruins observed.

On Kodiak, the largest of Alaska's many southern islands, are found the grandest of the brown bears. Feeding on salmon rich in protein, coastal female bears can reach 675 pounds or more and exceptional males can weigh as much as 1,400 pounds and reach nine feet tall standing on their hind feet.

This fork of the Thumb flowed into Karluk Lake in this somewhat southwestern portion of the island. Our camp, where we slept in rustic, native-owned cabins on Karluk's Camp Island, was less than a mile away by small skiff.

Part of Scott's job was to drop us off ashore, and clad in hip waders, position the raft away from the bank before joining us. This simple step discouraged the bears from approaching the raft while we were away and wreaking havoc on stowed gear, especially the life vests. Aside from that important duty, he prepared tasty meals and shared his vast understanding of the bears that we would encounter each day.

This small island's only other tenant was the US Fish and Wildlife Service. On the other side of the island from us, a couple of biologists seasonally lodged in a small, trashy cabin and flew out in an almost *toy-like*, two-seater plane to periodically monitor bear movements in this region. Their small holding along the shore gave evidence of many years of government spending, which had resulted in a heap of rubble around a decaying structure where they stayed.

Our purpose in making the long journey from home in the Lower Forty-Eight (or in Alaskan-speak, from "outside") to Kodiak was to enhance our understanding of this prime brown bear habitat. This knowledge would better enable us to assist the nearby native community of Old Harbor on the southeastern rim of the island with an ecotourism effort through GBF.

The term "ecotourism," popular in the mid-nineties, aptly described what all of us were striving to establish: an environmentally friendly approach to limited visitation to the region in the pursuit of bears, which in turn would produce a stable income base for the locals.

We had made our way from the beach through tall vegetation to a high point above the river, ever vigilant for bears snoozing in the lush vegetation that they would compact with their massive frames. Each daily walk from the raft to our viewing position would bring us close to several large bruins who gave a casual but convincing glance as we passed each of them sprawled among the grasses.

At the end of the worn path, we would take our places on a small, elevated wooden platform built by the native land owners expressly for bear viewing. There, we would engage in "bear watching" and soft discussions of our observations of bear interactions and feeding strategies.

Such viewing platforms were also found at other popular Alaskan bear gathering places, such as the Brooks River and McNeil River sites. The Brooks is found within Katmai National Park and Preserve, headquartered at King Salmon, 290 air miles southwest of Anchorage. McNeil River flows through McNeil River State Game Sanctuary and drains into Kamishak Bay, 250 air miles also southwest of Alaska's largest city.

These publicly managed sites allow a limited number of observers the unique opportunity to view nature at her best from safe vantage points. Viewing platforms located at these sites have long been respected by both bears and people.

The bears, over time, have become comfortable with the human intrusions within their prime fishing locations, and the viewers are carefully instructed and herded onto the platforms to make sure nothing that could be perceived as a threat by the bears occurs. In this manner, both bruin and man know their boundaries and respect each other's space. Our viewing location was unique in that it was on private land owned by Koniag, Inc., the regional native corporation of Kodiak Island.

In my visits there over a two-year period, we came to call the bank above the Thumb with its wooden platform "the bench." Located a mere dozen or so feet above the narrow river, the bench provided a great location from which to observe many bears. It was elevated enough to place observers above the river's bank vegetation, and it allowed us to have a 180-degree view of the river as it ran from east to west, emptying into Karluk Lake.

The bench also provided a comparable view behind us so that we periodically scanned for bears that might approach us from the rear through the underbrush. They were a curious lot, and it was not uncommon to have one or more bears investigate our intentions during the course of the day.

As the years would pass and I realized that I probably would never return to the bench, I often would wonder how I could have ever become bored and taken a nap on the wooden platform when many of nature's finest creations were just below me. Nonetheless, after several hours of gazing at these natural wonders as they selectively fed on the bounty of salmon, it was quite easy to drift off to sleep periodically with binoculars still in hand.

Strange as that reflection would seem, it was just a fact that we would see so many bears over the hours on each visit that I would become saturated with the awe of it all. Oh, to go back there, and again become restless with such repetition!

On this particular day, we had settled in for the morning on our perch, each of us finding just the right spot to position ourselves for optimal viewing, and all of us within a few feet of the weapons we had brought along. I had laid my belongings on the platform nearby alongside the shotgun that I owned. I scanned the terrain to our backside for anything of interest.

It was a sound that I would never forget!

The noise was not unlike one made by a car window that is not quite closed—a low, hissing sound. I had moved only feet away from the others who were gathered with me on the bench as I stooped toward the ground to retrieve my camera from the fanny pack near my feet.

Startled, I rather quickly looked from a crouched position to my right in the direction of *that hissing sound*. My eager eyes brought into focus at least two, maybe three, chocolate fuzzballs dwarfed by an immense adult bear form.

Slightly in front of two equally diminutive siblings, a brown bear cub only weeks old had hastily retreated at the sight of me only ten feet away. There followed a comical—but still serious—domino effect as the two others toppled into the much larger figure behind them.

I slowly and cautiously came to an upright position, totally unaware of how the other men, also potentially in harm's way, might be reacting to this intense moment. My focus immediately changed from the tiny cubs to the enormous protective mother bear only steps away.

She had risen above the bank of the river below the platform. In an almost surreal way, she stood there as all three retreating cubs squealed in fear at their discovery of me and withdrew to her for answers.

Female brown bears willingly take on much larger male bears in defense of their young. Male brown bears are known to kill and eat cubs, and females will fight to the death to protect their offspring. Therefore, there is little expectation that they will retreat from humans should their cubs become endangered. By far, the most feared bear encounter is a close one with a mother and her young, and that was exactly our situation...

The inquisitive mother now loomed over us from behind—a sizeable, well-nourished bear. Her determination and ability to defend her cubs was unmatched by our presence and our firepower.

As she eased up the bank, her massive, dark figure supported an enormous head that slowly swayed from side to side as if to put every sensory device into motion. Nothing escaped her fixed dark eyes, perked ears, and keen sense of smell. She was completely focused on assessing any threat to be addressed in defense of her offspring.

Slowly, she surveyed our presence to determine what had startled her vulnerable young family. Driven by instinct crafted over centuries of survival by her species, she methodically evaluated what reaction was appropriate, as I stood motionless in her shadow. Outside my peripheral vision, the others in my group remained firm yet tense in her presence.

Bigger than life, she stood with the sun behind her, outlining every feature of her gigantic frame against the skyline. A radiant glow appeared to accent her coat, and to me in this precarious circumstance, she seemed to eclipse the sun. I can recall an almost euphoric feeling, like an out-of-body view of the entire scenario for these mere seconds, but it quickly gave way to fear of what might happen next.

Her presence was overwhelming, for she was an astonishingly beautiful fortress. With no time to give the slightest thought to an escape plan and nowhere to retreat anyway, the outcome to this too-close encounter was, without question, the bear's decision. Nature would rule here, and how the day ended would be hers to decide!

What seemed like an *e-t-e-r-n-i-t-y* passed in anticipation of how this mother bear might respond, yet in retrospect, it was momentary. Her senses meticulously processed the necessary information, and she carefully determined that, while the cub's discovery of us was startling to them, we were not a threat to her young.

Without any appearance of doubt in her ability to deal harshly with us, she slowly eased down the bank and returned to the river with grace and confidence. The three brown fuzzballs hastily tagged along amiably and without any further display of emotion.

For reasons that would never be revealed to us, she had chosen to take her startled cubs and retreat rather than deal forcefully with the intrusion. Perhaps this was the cubs' first human encounter but a hapless repeated offense to their mother and unworthy of the energy required for engagement.

Had she chosen to attack, being mere steps away, we would have found ourselves helpless, despite the presence of a Winchester Police Riot stainless-steel 12-gauge shotgun lying on the ground nearby and a holstered Ruger Red Hawk .44 magnum—common gear on such outings. Powerful weapons, even in the grip of experienced shooters, are no assurance against the swift charge of a large bear at close range. Native Alaskans and informed users of the backcountry pack firearms as commonly as they don their "Tufs." (ExtraTufs™ were a brand of knee-high rubber boots popular throughout Alaska among seamen, anglers, and hikers for negotiating soggy, uneven tundra.) However, a high-caliber firearm is no substitute for sound judgment when facing a potentially lethal animal at close range.

It is difficult for a skilled marksman to make a killing shot at a charging force with the speed and agility of an angry bear. Bears can travel over 30 miles per hour, and even at a distance of 50 yards, an intruder finds himself with mere seconds to respond successfully. That is, if the threat is even detected in its approach.

This mother bear likely had even sensed our presence as we left Camp Island for this observation point. While small groups of observers from all over the world paid handsomely to stay in cabins on the smaller island and experience this guided feeding frenzy during the late summer salmon runs, these massive bruins passively tolerated their trespass.

Human scent noted and processed from hundreds of yards away generally gave little cause for alarm among browns experienced with alien intruders of their fishing grounds. After all, this was their land, and they knew how to defend it.

The bears' sense of smell no doubt alerted them to each daily human visit far ahead of visual recognition, and they generally paid little attention to our intruding party. Even the unmistakable roar of an Alaskan Beaver floatplane, with pontoons skimming the waters as it ferried paying viewers in or out of our camp, seldom drew a nod from the bears' mid-afternoon napping.

A concern on this visit—and subsequent trips from the skiff to the bench and back—was the unlikely event of startling a dozing bear curled up in the vegetation along the hundred-yard trail and going unnoticed until that surprise close encounter was imminent. There was a real possibility that such a situation would result in a charge with a potentially unpleasant outcome.

Each passage through this gauntlet of waist-high vegetation demanded our utmost attention to the landscape around us, and for me especially, as a novice walking among these giants, resulted in a firm grip on the 12-gauge.

This was an experience of a lifetime. I would often reflect on just how close we may have come to a frightening end. For the cubs, no doubt, it was a lesson early in life as to the smell and appearance of a less formidable creature.

Experienced with bears as we all were, I would forever recall this as one of those lucky days, with the only unpleasant outcome being the warm, yellow liquid that had accumulated about our feet and beckoned to be emptied from our Tufs.

CHAPTER 2

Goldilocks and the FOUR Bears

Those dark forms were not our friends!

*We had just realized that our group was not still inside the
shelter when the dark form lunged against the partially
opened gate. Hearts pounded and fright overcame our
weariness from the climb back up the hill as we gazed at
each other for a decision on what to do.*

Bob was *always* good for a bear. From the first time we hiked
together, there had been a bear encounter of some sort
involving Bob, usually up close and a little too personal. There was
just something about this internist from Chattanooga that seemed
to attract bears.

It was late summer 1980 when Gayle Cooper, friend and Director
of Non-Credit Programs for the University of Tennessee at Knoxville,

called. Gayle was also UT's Director of the Smoky Mountain Field School, and she asked if I would lead an outing in the Smokies.

The fledgling field school was a cooperative effort between UT and the National Park Service of the neighboring Great Smoky Mountains National Park. She had cofounded the school along with the park's assistant chief of interpretation, Don Defoe, who would become my primary contact with the park. Don also became a treasured friend, for he was a true gentleman and an exemplary park ranger.

They developed a partnership between the university and park for educating visitors on the value and proper enjoyment of the park's varied resources. This effort would be accomplished through sessions comprised of one or more days spent in the wilderness learning with experts in various areas of natural history.

These experts, almost exclusively college and university professors, shared their knowledge and experience in both classroom and field settings with participants who would enroll through the university and pay a nominal fee. In reality, the park provided the setting, and the university supplied the instruction.

When I was contacted, the field school was just two years old and offered sessions from early spring to late fall. Four years before, I had shifted out of the classroom, where I was a biology professor at Roane State Community College, to a new administrative post. Roane State was just thirteen miles from my home in Roane County, Tennessee.

During my five years as the college's director of personnel and affirmative action, we hired Gayle Cooper's husband, Hank, to direct governmental grant programs. It was through Hank that I became acquainted with Gayle. We subsequently hiked some together over the years and shared a mutual love of outdoor adventure.

Gayle and Hank were great people, energetic and upbeat, as well as knowledgeable hikers. Gayle was an outstanding administrator, and I was flattered when she called me, deeming my meager credentials and experience at the time worthy of university status.

She may have been somewhat desperate regarding this particular August session, a five-day backpacking trip. Five participants of varying ages had signed up, and the intended hike leader, Branley Owen, had defected to Colorado in the aftermath of divorce. That left me, eager yet inexperienced, to lead a journey of this magnitude through some of the South's most rugged and remote terrain.

The route would make a loop beginning in Cades Cove, travel up Ledbetter Ridge to join the Appalachian Trail, then head eastward along the AT to Derrick Knob Shelter before backtracking to Cades Cove.

Branley was said to hold the record for hiking end to end the two-thousand-plus miles of the AT. The trail made its way from a southern terminus on Springer Mountain, Georgia, through fourteen states to the rocky summit of Mt. Katahdin in Maine. The strenuous jaunt up Springer began at Georgia's Amicalola Falls State Park and Lodge. To reach the top of Mt. Katahdin in Baxter State Park, one had to complete the most precipitous climb on the entire AT.

The story told was that Branley, as an army ranger, came back from the Vietnam War and completed the entire AT in seventy-three days and nights. Though we never talked, I was in the same room with him once at an outdoor store where he gave a presentation.

I like many over-achievers, he was described as thinking highly of himself. This was evident in my one and only encounter with him. Several years later, I was told that Branley had tragically died of a heart attack somewhere out West.

To this day, I doubt that most hikers making extraordinary claims actually walk every step past each blazed tree on the route. A "blaze" is a 2-by-6-inch painted marking found all along the 2,175-mile trail to direct hikers as they plod along its course. There are over 300,000 of them painted on trees, rocks, signposts, guardrails, pavement, and wherever else they are needed to clarify direction.

I am convinced there are many "yellow blazers," a nickname coined by honorable hikers and ascribed to those who take shortcuts, especially on highways. It is thought that many of them skip considerable sections of the trail to shorten the journey and save time.

Claiming to hike the trail averaging forty or fifty miles daily until completion is laughable. More surprising is that many people believe such stories. Those innocent in their belief of such feats simply have no real concept of the rugged terrain through which much of the trail passes. Perhaps, too, the inability to perform simple math calculations continues to plague them from grade school years, else they would never purchase a lottery ticket either.

Besides, why would anyone want to sprint the AT and miss its many gems, from natural beauty to interesting people and places, that simply cannot be savored in a near run? Its founders did not conceive the trail with that in mind.

Difficult, rocky terrain found in New Hampshire and Maine makes it impossible to move continuously averaging even twenty or so miles a day. Okay, so some super athlete might power-walk more enticing portions of the trail.

However, I believe in time such physical abuse of the musculoskeletal system would result in severe consequences for the feet, knees, and hips. Over my own journey, I saw enough hikers blow out their feet between Springer and the Smokies (challenging, but just 165 miles) because they carried too much weight and hiked too many miles each day.

Dr. Robert (Bob) Myers, an internist from Chattanooga would be on this field school session. Bob was several years my senior, and this was his first session as well. Through the ensuing years, Bob would be a frequent participant on field school trips that Kathy and I would lead and would become a cherished friend and mentor.

Though I had backpacked in this region prior to the field school trip, it was my first time to enjoy the splendor of late summer. Each day's walk, though hot and humid, brought new experiences and strengthened friendships, especially between Bob and me.

Bob returned in June 1981 to backpack the eastern section of the AT from Newfound Gap to Davenport Gap, which is a distance of about thirty miles. There were four other participants on this trip, including Judy White, a dental hygienist from Wisconsin. Both would join me the next summer to complete the park's western leg of the AT.

Like the eastern section, this western portion of the AT followed the state line between North Carolina and Tennessee from Newfound Gap, roughly at the park's central point. It terminated at Fontana Dam after meandering forty miles, including a pass over the shoulder of Clingmans Dome at 6,643 feet, the highest point on the entire Appalachian Trail.

Judy was a few years younger than I was; I had just turned thirty-two. Though of different ages and backgrounds, Bob, Judy, and I immediately bonded for an enjoyable second trip together in the park. Bob, being a specialist in the field of medicine, and Judy being a hygienist applied their attention to detail to every aspect of hiking.

Bob carried an external frame pack, common at the time, as did I, and everything was always arranged as if on a surgical tray. Whatever the need along the way, be it a length of dental floss to sew up a stuff sack or an extra bulb for the two-cell flashlight, Bob had spares arranged in an orderly fashion.

I never ceased to be amazed at just how much he could so tightly squeeze into that pack of his, and yet it never appeared in disarray or all that heavy. He always looked dapper carrying it and seldom appeared to sweat under the burden. Bob had a cheery disposition and was one to be counted upon to keep a group upbeat despite the challenges of backpacking these mountains.

Judy was more the novice hiker and cognizant of every leaf and stick that she passed, never overlooking the opportunity to examine a new stove or ask about the rating of someone's sleeping bag. She carried an external pack like mine that I had lent her. Judy seemed vulnerable out there despite the fact that she was a strong hiker and cautious in our pursuits together.

There is plenty of opportunity for serious injury, or even death, in hiking and backpacking, but by using good judgment and the right gear, the probability can be minimized significantly. The drive to the trailhead probably presents a greater risk for most enthusiasts.

On this excursion westward, we were to walk the ridgeline, with significant portions of it above five thousand feet. It certainly was not an easy stroll. This was a remote area of the park, and getting help for a serious injury could take some time. In addition, at the higher elevations, the weather could deteriorate rapidly and become fierce even during the warm summer months.

Park regulations require overnight campers to stay in established shelters while hiking the Smokies portion of the AT. There were thirteen shelters along the seventy-mile route of the AT in the park at the time (Birch Spring Gap shelter has since been removed, and the site has been converted to a tent camping area). Each of them is spaced about five to seven miles apart, or a day's backpack for most travelers of this challenging terrain.

Despite the regulations, we would commonly witness one or more tents perched outside some of the more accessible shelters on any given night. The perpetrators knew that the risk of a ranger visit and a resulting citation was next to nil. The benefit to our party was a less crowded shelter.

Spence and Russell Fields were less than three miles apart, and a shelter was located at each of these popular destinations. Here, the trail was a moderate series of challenges crossing the enjoyable Little Bald at about midpoint between the two. Today, the hiker bypasses that section altogether on a much more pleasing and easier reroute completed several years ago with the help of our friend Bill Williams, who worked as an AT trail crew volunteer.

Hiking the western section now, I miss the view into North Carolina that was afforded by Little Bald, but I do not regret the more wearisome rocky walk that we had to endure on the former route. Besides, the vegetation on the slope beneath the Bald had grown to such a height over time that it significantly reduced the visibility of the Carolina mountains below.

After an uneventful night at Spence Field, our group arrived at the Russell Field shelter around noon. Some of the group needed to water up before hiking the next five miles to Mollie's Ridge for the night.

My knowledge and experience today would never permit a group to divide and part of them to go ahead while others sought water, but that was then. In my failure to address the issue of staying together, Bob and the others waited for a time and then decided to go on to the next shelter as Judy and I filled our water bottles further down the side trail toward Cades Cove.

Realizing that we were in bear country, and with good intentions, they hung our packs inside and secured the feeble chain closure on the shelter's gate before traveling onward. These were red Kelty® Tioga 1975 vintage external frame packs, among the better designs of their time.

It took considerable time for the two of us to obtain water, because the customary watering hole that I knew of below the shelter was almost dry. We had to travel a greater distance downhill to a source alongside this trail. It was a steep descent of maybe seventy-five yards from the original destination, and then about thirty-five yards more to the stream. Returning up a steep hill with our water bottles made for slow walking, and we stopped frequently to catch our breath.

Approaching the downhill side of the shelter, we thought of Bob and our fellow hikers awaiting us. Distracted by heavy breathing from the grind up the hill and meaningless conversation, we focused little on the commotion within the shelter. From maybe forty feet away, I cast an eye toward the shelter's opening and saw what my lethargic mind processed as one of our group shaking crumbs from a plastic bag through a slightly opened gate.

After a few steps more, Judy and I suddenly came to the realization that the movement at the shelter entrance was not from our group at all—it was from a sizeable bear inside the shelter!

What we had just seen before us was a mother bear thrashing a food bag from one of our packs as her three cubs, also inside, explored the other spoils. We had what is called "a situation"—four bears inside the shelter with the gate still chained but sprung open.

Those dark forms were not our friends!

Fear overwhelmed us, and rightfully so, because we now stood a short distance from the shelter gate, and if the mama bear had squeezed in, she could squeeze out at any moment. Hearts pounded and disbelief overcame each of us as we looked at one another for a clue about what to do. In retrospect, I wonder who was likely more frightened, the bears or us?

Immediately I thought that if one or more bears came through the partially chained shelter doorway this close, they would certainly charge us. On this discovery, too, more than one bear could be heard, as they must have realized their predicament.

Their sounds exploded into unsettling grunts and characteristic huffing sounds from the distress. We had inadvertently cornered them and they were coming out!

With minimal bear experience at this point in my career, I determined that our safest retreat would be to make our way behind the shelter quickly, out of sight of the agitated bear family. We would give the front side of the shelter a wide berth and climb up on the roof that sloped low toward the ground.

Hastily and clumsily, but with sufficient motivation, we aided each other in making our way onto the metal roof. The bears could be heard below, as some no doubt continued to explore our belongings while others rushed to escape from the building. In the process, one of our packs would be hurled to the dry, dusty, dirt floor while the other was spun around on its tether, and both would be lathered with bear slobber and ripped with sharp teeth.

In the 1970s, everyone wore heavy, leather hiking boots weighing three to four pounds a pair and overbuilt even for backpacking the rugged Southern Appalachians. We put these hefty tools to good use on the shelter's roof. Since for the moment we were out of harm's way on our metal-clad perch, we stomped up and down to make as much noise as possible. We thought this racket might drive the bears out of the shelter and away so that we might retrieve what was left of our packs and be on our way. It worked. Well, sort of.

Regaining our composure and even feeling a bit cocky, this became lame entertainment for us, despite what we expected to find if we ever did see the packs again. The frantic mother bear and her three cubs finally managed to squeeze back out through the partially opened gate and bolted down the bank adjacent to the shelter.

Trailing behind them was a whirlwind of plastic bags and food wrappers from provisions that were intended to last us two more days. Down the hillside the siblings hastily scurried in a tight wad with their mother in the lead as they disappeared into summer's greenery.

Victors, we quickly made our way down from the roof and raced for the same opening into the shelter from which the bear family had managed to escape. We did this without any thought of whether the gate was sprung open enough to allow us inside. This was not without our crashing face-to-face into each other, water bottles flailing and my camera strung about my neck swinging wildly out of control.

Squeezing through the narrow opening, we struggled to close the gate behind us and secured it with a piece of loose chain. It had not been spread more than a foot or so but somehow had allowed a full-grown adult bear and her progeny to pass through. I have not yet been able to envision how all four of them managed to get inside and then back out through such a narrow passage.

We surveyed the pack damage, and though slight, both packs would require a trip back to their manufacturer for repairs of the

Cordura® packcloth. More disturbing at the moment was the slobber—bear slime and trail grit—that enveloped each pack end to end. Every morsel of food had been crudely removed by hungry mouths.

As we were coming off the high from the experience, the female bear and her offspring climbed back up the hillside. They made their way to the front of the shelter and began pawing at the bottom of the gate to get back to the goodies where the two of us huddled inside.

Since I hiked with a hefty dogwood stick, I began poking it through and under the fence in a feeble attempt to drive the determined bears away. Several prods accompanied by intense yelling proved successful for the moment, and they departed once again down the hillside.

Next, we gathered several rocks from outside the gate and from inside where campers had used them around the fireplace. As the mother and her eager followers returned up the bank, I stepped outside and unleashed a barrage of projectiles, missing more than making contact.

In this determined effort, I did not want to hurt the bears but rather to startle them enough to send them on their way. It seemed cruel to assault a bear with a rock, especially a young one, despite the fear that they instilled and the damage our gear had incurred.

I found it intriguing that when I occasionally connected a rock with the reappearing mother and her brood, she did not seem to make the association between the insult and me, the defender of our space. With the ensuing attempt to win ground, I became more successful in making contact. Finally, deciding to avoid the calamity, they ventured off down the hill a third time—for good.

At least an hour had passed by now, and certainly the others would reach our evening's destination of Mollie's Ridge well before us. We surveyed the damage, cleaned off our packs as best we could, and restuffed everything that had been removed by inquiring snouts. Not a trace of food remained, but astonishingly, damage to the packs did not preclude their further use.

The five-mile hike to rejoin our group at Mollie's allowed time for us to consolidate our thoughts on what we had just witnessed. We came to realize that what had been a remarkable experience could have resulted in serious injury, or worse, had the frantic mother bear burst from the shelter into the two of us. A female with cubs will defend them from any perceived threat, and she will do so without hesitation or concern for herself.

It only took this one encounter to change forever the manner in which I approached a shelter. This experience taught me when arriving at a shelter or campsite area to be vigilant and to make plenty of noise. There was always the possibility that an inattentive bear could be inside the shelter or scavenging nearby for whatever treats were left behind by careless packers.

Upon arriving at Mollie's Ridge shelter, we were promptly greeted by Bob and the balance of our group with a look of concern for our delayed arrival. With grim faces we pivoted around to display our bedraggled dirty packs. They all peered in astonishment at the crusty, tattered packcloth with its obvious damage from curious jowls.

With a story fabricated and tweaked over the five miles, we told of how we were attacked by bears from behind as we sought to catch up with our group. The yarn spun out of control when we recanted how we fought them off, narrowly escaping death, before finally reaching our destination. Eventually, but quicker than we had hoped, they were on to us. We were forced to give up the truth.

What at the moment was a feeling of fear and vulnerability became a rather exciting testimony on bear and human interaction. This story would be shared repeatedly with more emphasis on the antics of the bears than on the hilarity of the human subjects in solving their dilemma.

Bob had proven his talent as a bear magnet. Though he was not present during our encounter, we credited him with the lure of the bruins to these woods.

Judy, with her charming, mid-length golden hair, had brought to reality Goldilocks and the *FOUR* bears!

CHAPTER 3

Buster and the Berry Patch

Just as surprised as we were, the black figure centered in the berry patch jerked upright and seemed to stare through us with intense, dark eyes. There was little doubt what would happen next.

Days would be spent in July and August atop the Smokies between Spence and Russell Fields, two historic balds important as summer livestock grazing grounds to the early pioneer settlers of these misty Southern Appalachian mountains.

We had decided that we would backpack there in hopes of seeing bears, though it would be stiflingly hot and muggy, even at five thousand feet. This was within Great Smoky Mountains National Park, and both areas boasted primitive, backcountry shelters where hikers were required to lodge should they stay overnight.

The Appalachian Trail bisects this impressive International Biosphere Reserve along its mountainous spine as it makes its way along the crest end to end with North Carolina to the east and Tennessee to the west. It meanders up and over Spence Field and connects to Russell Field by an improved section of the AT, where it crosses the ridge adjacent to the bald there.

Streams at both locations were vital resources for cattle, sheep, and goats that once grazed there. Since both areas had sources of water, they also became popular hiking and horseback riding destinations long before the park was established in 1934.

Called "fields," "upland meadows," and "balds," these high elevation features generally have sparse growth and an openness unique among the mountainous ridges lush with temperate deciduous foliage. Perhaps the term "bald" was derived from observing their intermittent tree cover from a higher point, where the site below appeared as a head with little hair.

Some claim they came about due to fires initiated by lightning or formed as a result of Native Americans periodically setting fire to them. Others theorize that excessive livestock grazing may have played an important role. Though their origin is unknown, they often provide hikers and horseback riders with breathtaking, panoramic views with layers of distant mountains.

This summer, we would encounter a number of bears frequenting these open meadows to climb their much sought-after serviceberry trees for the tasty fruits of late summer.

I often thought of it as a natural pruning process when I saw where bears had broken their branches perusing the diminutive trees for food. Some branches would be ridden to the ground, thereby allowing bears to stand on their hind feet and enjoy the ripe burgundy-colored delights. The feeding frenzy left every productive tree comically splayed and void of fruit by season's end.

Early settlers referred to these trees, members of the rose family, as "sarvis" and treasured the annual berry harvest for juice and jelly. Sarvis actually was a slang version of "service" and is said to have referred to the circuit rider's preaching services that came with spring and the display of the serviceberry's showy white flowers.

Sarvis branches were also said to have been used to decorate churches during revivals or to adorn caskets in funeral services for those who did not survive the harsh winters. There were many services during the period in which these mountains were settled, and some individuals simply starved to death if winter hung on too long.

After parking just beyond the park's Cades Cove Campground entrance station, we would frequently make our journey through the woods and across the creek to the adjoining picnic area several hundred feet away. It seemed that we always had difficulty finding our way from the parking lot to the neighboring roadway, though the vegetation really was not that dense. We reasoned that this was due to the abundance of confusing paths etched out by the hordes of tourists, who for the most part were clueless of their own destinations.

It never failed that we came out off course from where we had projected our travels would take us. When we led group trips, we would walk the pavement from the entrance station, traveling the road we came in on until it joined with the road into the picnic area. This walk was a rather circuitous route to the trailhead but it avoided the embarrassment of the trip leaders getting lost.

This popular and thus shamefully overused picnic area seemed to host several thousand "Michigan Yankees," among others, throughout the summer. Ignoring the plethora of government information warning of bears in the park, they naively would spread their fare onto the myriad concrete tables on sunny weekend days.

Of course, this often meant exceptional dining for some of the savvier bruin that dwelled in the area and knew how to work the system. As a bonus, the ensuing mayhem provided entertainment for the more experienced folks frequently dining adjacent to them.

The system was to allow sufficient time for the traditional Coleman® cooler to be emptied onto the table—fried chicken, mandatory; potato salad from MamMaw's old recipe; baked beans that would have every car window opened to its fullest before the family left for home from the park boundary; coleslaw; and all sorts of cholesterol-laden snacks and fattening deserts that would hurl any picnicker or bear into drooling Pavlovian reflex.

About the time the dogs came off the charcoal from the overbuilt and certainly overpriced government grill, the bear or female and cubs would make their customary pitch by rushing the scene and sending even the elderly scampering to a nearby restroom as a safe haven.

It was not uncommon for some brave soul to attempt to defend the table, but they, too, would soon be dispatched to the privy by a series of intimidating lunges and huffs from these skilled panhandlers. Then the party would begin!

All four bear paws would be placed at center table, trashing the impressive layout, while an eager snout sampled every delight. And of course, the lid had to be ripped from the Coleman® just to make sure nothing edible had escaped their keen sense of smell. No doubt the display of strength also was to affirm who ruled this wood.

The next phase of this scenario played out when a green uniform arrived to chase the bruin away and allow the still-shaken visitors a quick bear-butt picture of the escape. In this manner, they could return to Michigan (not always Michigan, but always Yankees) with positive proof that they had conquered one of nature's most unruly and savage beasts.

The reality was that the bear would become more confident; intensify the aggressive behavior on future encounters; and in all likelihood would be euthanized by the rangers after another episode.

Sadly, established management protocol dictated that repeat offenders be destroyed, for the risk of injury to visitors was too great. Besides, black bears were plentiful.

The tourists were at fault. They essentially destroyed what they came to see by not abiding by park regulations and using good judgment while a visitor to bear habitat. After all, the bears had free range, and the temptation of an easy meal was too seductive to resist.

A careful survey of the area prior to making the noon meal spread might have discovered an eagerly waiting bear nearby. A more conservative approach to spreading the fare, not to have too much food out at any given time, could have reduced the alluring scent and visual enticement to an interested bear family. And finally, it would have been prudent to have gathered a small stack of rocks for hurling at a distant bear before it could gain control of the scene.

These simple steps might have prevented the ruination of an otherwise peaceful outing in the Smokies. Once a bear that has been conditioned to "people food," it loses its fear of humans, and it is too late to change its predictable path to destruction.

I always drew a sigh of relief when we pressed past the gate of the gravel roadway upon leaving the picnic area where we would begin our five-mile climb up to the balds. There was something about having to walk through this maze of weekend nature-lovers that one just knew were clueless about wilderness and its needs when we were off to backpack into its core.

Peace would not be fully attained before passing a few hundred more feet along this gravel thread and beyond a horse staging area. From here, more locals than Yankees would leisurely ride up on horseback to where we were headed, afoot and under the burden of our backpacks.

As they would pass our sweaty figures, we often cringed, for at least one horse in every small posse would struggle under the load of an obese rider. All lathered up, they would plod along under the duress of some Southerner who had never graced a gym since public school and at breakfast had delighted in porking down plates of biscuits and gravy for the entire course of their life.

Generally, backpackers have little use for horse folks when they ignore backcountry etiquette. We once witnessed the carnage left behind by horseback riders at Cosby Knob shelter just off the AT in the most eastern region of the park. These visitors had taken the liberty of scattering an abundance of soiled paper plates, plastic ware, and other assorted trash into the woods below the shelter after their meal. They did this rather than carry out their litter on horseback.

The first stretch of this day's journey was easy, for it followed a woods road with only a slight gain in elevation. After a little more than a mile and a half, forking at a clearing, the trail split to the north (left) leading up to Spence Field and to the south (right) to Russell Field.

Often we would stop for lunch in this opening, where yellow poplars towered over strewn boulders that offered seating above damp ground. The gray-barked Tennessee state trees were early successional cover that soon established a new forest after fire or clear-cutting.

Intense logging had reduced this entire region to shambles of eroded hillsides in the late 1880s and early 1900s prior to park establishment. It was really quite amazing how the forest had recovered in less than a hundred years.

Some logging activity continued within the park until around 1937, based on prior agreements and after the 1,200 families had been woefully displaced by the government's use of the power of eminent domain. Big government's greater-good ploy was used often as well for Tennessee Valley Authority acquisitions at the turn of the century.

The insult was no different when decades before Native Cherokees had been booted out of these same lands by early white settlers and senselessly death-marched westward on the Trail of Tears. While these isolated settlers did not enjoy the many benefits of a prospering commerce outside their coves, for many life was good back in these hills, and government intervention was not welcomed.

As a result of this being a popular lunch stop for most hikers to either of the two destinations, we often would see yellow government postings that warned of recent bear encounters. I thought it humorous that often such signs showed obvious indications of bear tooth marks.

Even then, early in our bear experiences, we quickly learned to sit in opposing directions while partaking our lunch to make sure we were not surprised by a meandering bear knowledgeable of this honey spot. This simple technique of sitting back to back gave the two of us a visual of the complete circle of forest around us.

After lunch, the next three or so miles up to either Spence or Russell always proved more challenging on a full stomach. Indulging on too much chocolate could dispatch the offender laden with a heavy pack more than once into the bushes for relief before making the ridge top.

The hike up to Spence Field, after the trail joined the old Bote Mountain Road, was on an eroded path through rhododendron tunnels. Exacerbating the agony of hiking the incline was the underlayment of coarse rocks that wreaked havoc on tiring feet.

It was said that the road was originally named Vote Mountain because the Cherokee Indians used it to travel over the mountain to vote when they were granted that right. Since the Cherokee language had no "V" sound, the road became known as Bote Mountain Road. Makes a good story, but there is some doubt as to its authenticity.

Pioneer inhabitants of Cades Cove seasonally herded their stock to the higher grounds to graze on the rich grasses of the balds during the long summer months. The air was cool, and the hillsides wept with occasional springs that provided water for both herders and their stock.

Equestrians and "two-footers" shared several of the more than eight hundred miles of trails within the park, and hikers generally held little appreciation for horses. After a rain, it would be quite obvious that four hooves damaged the trails far more than the Vibram soles of two hefty leather boots and a wooden hiking stick common to the era.

The last half mile before topping out at the Appalachian Trail on the Spence Field approach was even more eroded and wound through an interesting corridor of dense rhododendron shrubbery. It always seemed that no matter the time of year or day, this walk was depressingly shaded and foggy. This created an eerily dark gauntlet that had been carved out by countless early wagon-travelers and livestock.

Though I do not ever recall encountering a bear on our numerous hikes up to Spence (and Russell) fields, I always expected to be "woofed" at some point along this last rhododendron-shrouded stretch. Had I been born a bear, it certainly would have been viewed favorably as a human ambush site not to be passed up.

Walking a short distance on the AT west and upward toward a knoll, we would take the short side trail down to the Spence Field shelter for the night's stay. Upon arriving, we were always exhausted from the climb's three-thousand-foot gain in elevation, and our clothes would be soaked with sweat.

Aside from our labor, we attributed the wetness to the high humidity during the months of July and August. Why we ever hiked anywhere in the South then I cannot comprehend. The weighty packs that we justified for mostly overnight stays in a shelter no doubt amplified our wet, salty state.

Our packs often weighted forty to fifty pounds, containing not so much food as gear that we always thought we might need. These were Kelty® Tioga, expedition packs, mine red and Kathy's light blue in color, with more than ample capacity for an overnighter but filled each time to the max.

They were constructed with aluminum external frames about which the pack body was fastened. This design feature would be reversed in years to come, placing the support frame inside the pack cloth and close to the back.

It has always been my opinion that this was a move based purely on marketing strategy rather than logic. External frames allowed a breathing space between the pack and one's back, and most had several outside pockets for the convenient location of needed items.

Internal frame packs, with their hidden supports riding closer to the back, allow for little evaporation of perspiration and tend to be one big bag where everything makes its way to the bottom. Also, an external frame pack remained erect for retrieval of gear when leaned against a tree. An internal frame pack will simply collapse into a heap.

Before huffing it the remaining four hundred or so feet down to the shelter, we turned left to go out onto the Spence bald for a view. We were ready for a reward for the hard climb. This well-worn section of the AT would take us slightly uphill through spotty stands of mountain laurel (pioneers called it ivy) dwarfed by serviceberry trees.

Now in a relatively open space and still catching our breath, we were not thinking of bears but more of self-worth and gratitude for being so close to our evening's destination. After all, no matter how many times we would make this journey, it was an arduous feat worth celebrating when we finally made it to the top.

The reward for hiking these five miles was the 360-degree view one had, peering into North Carolina and Tennessee from this domed landscape, where only distant signs of human encroachment could be detected across endless layers of smoky mountains.

The "smoke" resulted from transpiration, or the release of water vapor as a byproduct of respiration, from millions of plants that made these eight hundred square miles their habitat. The humidity that we loathed came from this same "smoke."

There was a healthy, unique stand of heath shrubs that hugged the trail's left side where we made our way up toward the bald's highpoint.

In early green summer coat or in fall's changing hues, this plot was distinguishable from all others. Tasty dark berries were always abundant here in late summer and blanketed the shrubbery. It was at this spot on this particular day that we would encounter "Buster."

Still laboring to breathe and discussing why we ever made this wretched climb once, and certainly questioning our sanity for making multiple trips here in the heat of summer, we suddenly came face-to-face with a feisty young bear.

Just as surprised as we were, the black figure jerked upright about thirty feet to our front amidst what was evidently *his* berry patch. Now fully alert to our presence and rigid, the bear cast dark eyes upon our sweaty figures as if he had seen his first humans.

At this point in our hiking tenure, our knowledge of bear behavior was limited. Certainly, our number of actual encounters was scant, and all of our field experiences had been from a safe distance.

Though standing side by side, we seemed almost unaware of the other's presence, paralyzed at the sight of that bear so close to us. Panic overtook the need to communicate our predicament to each other. The anticipated outcome of this confrontation proved too intense for either of us to remain steadfast.

Likewise, Buster probably lacked experience on how he should view such two-legged aliens. In an instant, he would explode from that berry patch at full charge toward our wet, salty figures burdened with the red and blue humps on our backs.

We had savored many stories by this point in our outdoor experiences. We had memorized the what to do and what not to dos when encountering bears. Never turn and run was paramount in the protocol. Running from a bear is thought to instill an instinctive predator-prey reflex that has resulted in mauling and even human death. At this point, there had never been a bear-caused human fatality in the Smokies, even though the park hosted millions of visitors every year.

Both of us had repeatedly processed this knowledge and discussed ad nauseam how we would react to a close encounter. Moreover, on many drives to the park we had rehearsed in our minds just such a scenario as this.

However, knowledge and logic seemed to depart from us like the wind as we gazed in fright. Informed and confident of our understanding as we were, we turned 180 degrees and *ran like we were on fire!*

The swiftness of our retreat was compromised by our exhaustion and the weight we bore on our backs. The exasperation that we experienced from the relentless final approach of our climb gave way to terror as we feared for our lives and bolted back down the path.

Instinct and no doubt the anticipated delightful entertainment of it all would direct Buster to do the same and strike out after the two of us. As if catapulted by some supernatural force, he arched from his patch, landed on all four paws, and bounded behind.

Bears have been recorded traveling over thirty miles per hour in a full charge, a speed that can easily overtake the fastest of humans. So there was no match here. There was only the perception that we were escaping and saving ourselves in this race against time.

From the onset, the weighty packs figured little in our thoughts of escape. Suddenly infused with perhaps gallons of adrenaline, fatigue took a backseat. Love for each other mattered not; it was clearly each one for themselves.

After probably less than forty yards, Buster broke the chase, snorted and huffed as agitated bears are wont to do, and loped off the hillside behind us and to our left. Our burdensome pace did not slow for some distance. We ultimately realized that the pursuit had ended as abruptly as it had begun and that we just might witness another day.

We came to a halt and over time regained a more normal heart rate and sought to restore our dignity. What a sight this must have been to young Buster, seeing two frail humans with loaded packs defy the laws of physics and flee at such an astonishing speed, believing they had won this race.

That bear was never seen again for the remainder of our overnight stay at Spence, or on any other subsequent adventures to these high-altitude meadows. We are confident still that Buster regrouped with more of his kin and recanted the story repeatedly of the idiotic two-leggers stumbling into his berry patch.

Forevermore, future visits up that knoll would mandate a pause and have us scope those heath shrubs, and reminisce our frightful encounter with Buster the bear.

Berry Patch Epilogue

Fast-Forward Fifteen Years

There was nothing noteworthy about our hike at this point. Our small band was finally arriving at the mountain crest where the Bote Mountain Road trail intersected the Appalachian Trail. As on many prior visits to these Smoky Mountains, we had gained significant elevation since we had left our vehicles in the cove some five miles below.

This humid August hike was conducted as an offering of the University of Tennessee and National Park Service Smoky Mountain Field School. Kathy and I were leading a group of participants on an overnight hike to Spence Field to enjoy a summer weekend of nature.

As on almost all hikes that we conducted, I would lead the group from the front and Kathy would encourage the stragglers at the rear. This system was not based on ego or ability, but rather on what seemed best to work for the two of us. I was taller and moved at a sporadic, faster pace with my longer legs, and Kathy enjoyed plodding along at a more constant speed.

Also, we had learned from earlier experiences in leading groups that one of us needed to be at the front. After all, we were responsible for our party's safety should we encounter any sort of danger (a rattlesnake?). Also, we had learned that stronger, more experienced participants seldom considered the frustration of those who struggled at a slower pace in attempting to keep up.

Being the leader has its rewards. On this particular trip, the most inspiring one was that a young girl, who had come along with her parent, seemed infatuated with the "professor," her leader. I found renewed energy in thoughts of her admiration and interest. She was a pretty teen who seemed enthralled with every word of wisdom that I could muster as I labored to maintain some normalcy in breathing so as not to appear affected by our precipitous climb. She followed close behind me every step of our journey.

As we reached the top of the mountain, we paused near the sign denoting the trail junction, and everyone finally gathered up into a small huddle, anticipating an announcement of our next move. I suggested a view from the top of Spence Field before turning back west toward the short trail down to the shelter where we would spend the night.

Eager to be able to return home and say, that they had hiked on the Appalachian Trail, everyone fell into single file behind my recently acquired admirer. Never passing up an opportunity to relate a tale about one of our many previous adventures, I began to relate the story of Buster the bear and his berry patch. Not everyone could hear my oratory, but that mattered not. It was only important that my new friend became excited as she absorbed the drama that I played out while we walked.

My story came to the part where I told of Buster bursting forth from his feeding grounds just as we approached that same berry patch. There was no cause for the anticipation that the event would repeat itself some years later; what were the chances of that?

As the two of us now walked side by side, since the trail widened, suddenly and without the slightest sound a bear similar in size to Buster bolted upright among those same heath shrubs!

I stood in rigid amazement as my young friend immediately pivoted around for a run back down the trail from where we had come. Wiser and more experienced by this point, I firmly grasped her arm and quietly insisted that she remain in place. She was too frightened to argue, though her trembling figure tensed in defiance.

In our firm stance we posed no threat or challenge for the young bruin. As quickly as we had seen the bear rise up on its two hind feet, it fell upon all four paws and disappeared as if it had never risen within this berry patch. The imposing dark figure was never seen again during our time at Spence.

As everyone interpreted what they had just witnessed and the young girl's gasp gave way to awe, their leader struggled inwardly to remain calm and unaffected by it all. It did not get much better than this—to stand steadfast and confident in the presence of a black bear while leading a bunch of novices who were still recovering from a rush of anxiety.

The story of Buster had set the stage: the new bear, not likely Buster years later, had appeared, and their trusted leader had shown no outward sign of surprise during the intrusion, much less fear. The entire event was only moments in duration, and yet it brought back years of experiences and reflections of prior encounters.

For the participants, this would be a hike, a place, and a leader that they would never forget, and they would retell the story at every opportunity. For the young admirer and me, certainly it was memorable; every bear experienced up close is. But more importantly, it etched in the minds of at least a few the need to remain calm and resist the urge to run from a bear.

For our youngest hiker, while the experience was terrifying at first, it would become a memory of a lifetime.

CHAPTER 4

Ghost of Resurrection River

There was not a print, no broken twigs, nothing—it had just vanished.

I was still several minutes from reaching the parking lot when I passively looked up from my flawed downward gaze on the trail. Like all hikers, I had become preoccupied with my destination rather than with my surroundings.

I drove my rental car into the small gravel parking area just before the bridge over Resurrection River and the sign just ahead announcing Kenai Fjord National Park's Exit Glacier.

Though seldom without Kathy, I was solo on this Alaska trip, scouting to renew our knowledge of favorite stopping points in the southeastern region. The Kenai, as it is known, is a peninsula approached from Anchorage by the Seward Highway forking to either the coastal village of Seward or down to Homer on the spit.

The Seward area, about 125 miles south of Anchorage, was one of our most anticipated destinations whenever we conducted small group trips. There was the surrounding Chugach Mountains, with their incredible lush green rising hills (we could always locate a bear or two on any one of them with the spotting scope), and then the seaport town of Seward itself. The friendly little town always bustled with fishing activities and has remained quaint despite an increase of tourist traffic over the years.

Anglers came from all over Alaska and the Lower Forty-Eight (or in the local vernacular, people from "outside") to gamble its frigid waters for halibut and kings. Never was a trip made to Seward during the fishing season that we did not encounter hordes of RVs and rows of truck-campers nestled tightly along the banks of this bayside town.

The highway entrance to the Kenai Fords Park was just before Seward. I stopped here to consider hiking a distance along the Resurrection River just to see what I might discover. Though we had been to Exit Glacier several times before, a solo hike along the river here would be a new venture.

From my parking lot vantage point, an obvious footpath extended into the black spruce, but it was soon swallowed up by the darkness of the forest. I sat for several minutes debating with myself (and losing) as to my own welfare should I consider going it alone through this gauntlet of high vegetation knowing what I might encounter, a bear or a moose.

I would be breaking my own rule to set out down an unfamiliar trail by myself in such wild country. In every outdoor presentation we had ever given, we had emphasized the potential hazards of hiking solo and extolled the many benefits of a small-group experience. Hiking with one friend or several not only provided a much higher degree of safety, but made the trip more enjoyable among those of similar persuasion. Nonetheless, the challenge of discovery overpowered reason.

Yes, the Ruger Redhawk was on my side, but it did not displace the higher safety margin of hiking with several friends. Nonetheless, I felt confident carrying the massive stainless steel cannon.

If later I were found reduced to a heap of bear poop among the spruce needles that littered the path, this analysis would prove flawed. Snubbing the rules we had preached ad nauseam would puzzle Kathy for the balance of her life, or at least until she found a savvier mate.

I did not relish the idea of my bones being ground-up by those sizeable molars that I had often pointed out on a bear skull, which we toted to educational sessions for emphasis. Nor did I want to dwell on what those last few conscious moments might be like in the clutches of an angry bear. Although the bears here were mostly black bears, they were *BIG* black bears! Putting those thoughts aside, I rationalized that hiking a short distance would somehow be okay.

I was preparing to get out of my vehicle when a recreational vehicle turned into the lot in front of me and came to a dusty halt after jostling the family of four along the gravel road. I hesitated to see just how this might play out.

In no time, two small figures dwarfed by massive daypacks erupted out the side door in obvious excitement of an impending hike and then raced down the path. They appeared to be the very young son and daughter of a mid-thirties couple who would take their time in donning packs, methodically securing their RV, and then following the children.

Immediately, the two tiny stick figures with their colorful packs, unconcerned in their innocence about the adults who lingered, were engulfed by the dense forest that lay ahead. The parents seemed oblivious to the potential threats found here, and lagged behind the children who were long out of sight by now.

I resisted the urge to yell, "You idiots, do you not realize that you are in bear country, and there are things out here that will eat you?" Squelching my rage at such stupidity and irresponsibility on the part of the caretakers of these precious mortals, I entertained another thought: *Bait!*

With the children a distance up front and the parents lingering behind, I would have two layers of bear bait in front of me should I decide to spend some time on this trail. Four warm bodies traveling ahead of mine should emit enough scent to send any large mammal nearby scurrying for cover. In addition, any bear or moose within a hundred yards and not deaf would clearly discern the giggling and chatter that streamed from these diminutive explorers.

Countering this urge to proceed, I evaluated the noise produced by the river as it flowed closely beside this narrow corridor of tall undergrowth neighboring each side of the trail. There really was the possibility that an animal would not smell or hear a person walking alongside because of the roar and breeze generated by these glacial-silted waters. A simpler, and perhaps less daunting, demise for the traveler would be to fall into the frigid water and lapse into hypothermia.

While this was not the best of circumstances for a hike alone, I reasoned that I would only walk a short distance and be especially vigilant. So, without further hesitation, I locked my rental and proceeded into the woods with the foursome well ahead and not in sight.

I would not call this an extraordinary walk on an Alaskan scale, but it was nice to be out. I thought too, that there must be something worthwhile about this trail, for it led six miles or so to a remote Forest Service cabin that could be rented for a minimal charge. As I walked this path, I noticed that huge growths of devil's club abounded on each side, nourished by the rich, moist soil.

Devil's club was said by my old friend and bear expert Chuck Jonkel to be good bear food. Being on the board of Great Bear Foundation with Chuck, I had been on several trips with him in search of bears. We would always find other treasures on which he also commented, such as various plants.

On one of those trips, several of us were stuffed in his old van racing down a dusty road on a journey to look for bears when he pulled alongside a stand of devil's club. Chuck abruptly stopped, got out of the vehicle, and dropped down the bank amidst the undergrowth, I thought to pee—again.

Rather, he knelt down under the immense foliage of this plant, which was new to me. With a pocketknife he always carried in tight jeans too youthful for his senior figure, he came up with a large stalk of the club where it attached at the base of the plant. It reminded me of an enormous celery stalk.

Unlike celery, though, it had threatening and evil-looking sharp spines along the entire length of the stem that demanded caution when handling. I thought to myself that the white, fleshy limb with its expanding base actually might be rather manageable and quite tasty.

Actually, Native Americans were said to seek the plant for food and medicinal purposes. Used for a long list of aliments, Alaska tribal natives nicknamed it "Tlingit aspirin," and its bright red fruit becomes bear candy in the fall.

This sighting was just another example of the all-around knowledge of natural history stored beneath Chuck's rumpled mass of white hair. It was one of many useful tidbits of knowledge that I would treasure from him during our jaunts together in Yellowstone and other parts of Montana.

Chuck was a character all right. His stocky, disheveled figure always shuffled through the woods with a slight limp, and his senior's gait I found amusing. He had a sense of humor, and it would always come out, no matter how seriously he prodded a piece of new bear data. He was funny, yet I held the greatest respect for his knowledge of wood lore and the bruins he loved and unceasingly ranted about protecting.

Reflecting back, I think ol' Chuck enjoyed the whimsical depiction by the casual observer of him as a grumpy gnome. Chuck was ever up for a tale, but he took seriously his self-imposed mandate to describe the bruin accurately to his faithful followers or those just curious about this man's point of view.

Chuck spoke with somewhat of a comical lisp that was said to have resulted from a frostbitten tongue, but I never quite found the right opportunity to ask about that. On a weekend gathering in the national forest outside of Whitefish, Montana—bear honorings, he called them—I came to understand how this might have happened.

After spewing forth hours of bear information too vital to forget and stories too remarkable to be anything but true, finally he would exhaust his once-eager audience, and they would stumble to their tents for relief.

Of course, this was around a roaring fire, where gallons of what he called "cowboy coffee" and an even greater amount of beer were consumed under stars too countless and brilliant to be anywhere but out West. I never dared to venture a look down the throat of that enormous coffee pot, for even at its cleanest, it would have sent any respectable health inspector off into the bushes, heaving.

Though I was impressed that at such gatherings Chuck insisted on a certain dishwashing routine, which included a rinsing of every utensil, cup, and dish in bleach water strong enough to tie-dye any shirt of the 60s. But I do not think that coffee pot *ever* saw soap or experienced an immersion in Clorox®.

Abandoned and left with only glowing ashes from a dwindling fire, Chuck would simply pile up in the leaves adjacent to a nearby tree under an old, ratty blanket retrieved from his cluttered van. He would commence this campsite ritual with what was not even a facsimile of a pillow and launch his "roar."

This was not the ordinary male bugle, but a deafening rattle that would defy the utterance of any bear. It came from an open mouth where, I theorized, his tongue could have been exposed for frostbite at some time prior. Sleeping no more than a few hours, he would have us all up again for more endless rants about how bureaucratic agencies had failed the bear (of course he was right) and that torturous cowboy brew that had thickened overnight on dying embers.

On my walk now along the Resurrection River, I wanted no part of this trailside growth of devil's club. I pondered the predicament, should I have to step off for a nature break. The trail through this impressive growth made for soft walking, for it was a bed of loose, dark soil covered with spruce needles and leaves. Had there been any footprints of wild creatures, I felt that they would easily have been spotted. Such thoughts drew repeated reflections upon the weapon carried at my side.

After walking some distance, I would occasionally get a glimpse of the family well ahead of me. Certainly I could detect sounds from the children, though they were overwhelmed by the river's rush, indicating their enjoyment of the walk.

When there was a clear view forward, I noticed every time that the parents were well behind the kids, without a clue of the potential danger to all of them. This still played in my favor and provided me the opportunity to keep walking with a certain degree of confidence in my safety.

In perhaps less than a mile, I could see the couple stop and regroup the children alongside them. After what seemed to be a discussion of whether or not to go any further while gesturing back in my direction, they retreated toward me. Continuing my progress onward, we soon faced each other for the first time.

It was interesting when the woman eventually saw my handgun how she changed her whole demeanor from friendly to alarmed composure. One would have thought she had seen an intergalactic alien. The thought of someone in her wilderness sporting a firearm obviously was foreign to her.

She had either never been around guns, had a bad experience with them at some point in her life, or as I suspected, felt fear out of ignorance of the need to be armed in such circumstances. She never spoke a word about this, but her focus during the brief conversation was fixed at my side. The husband and kids seemed oblivious and just eager to proceed back to their RV.

Their retreat from the forest now precipitated a decision on my part. To go on alone for any distance was not wise, but to retreat so soon seemed disappointing; so wisdom aside, I pressed onward. I reasoned that I would only go a little bit farther just to see if there was some reason that they had stopped. In less than a hundred yards, I guess, the terrain seemed much the same as what I had covered, so I turned around.

By this time, the family was well beyond sight or sound and had left my thoughts entirely. Even though I was enjoying this time with nature and liked the idea of seeing an occasional glimpse of the river, I became preoccupied with getting back to my rental car and proceeding on to Seward for the evening.

I had the options to camp bayside in Seward's public campground or stay in one of several tourist lodgings. I would choose to camp and enjoy this Alaskan experience oceanside. However, before that would become a reality, two strangers would come face-to-face, surprised!

I was still several minutes from reaching the parking lot when I passively looked up from my flawed downward gaze on the trail. Like all hikers, I had become preoccupied with my destination rather than with my surroundings. Within twenty to thirty yards of me, mid-trail, *a massive black bear just appeared!*

My initial thought about this bear (other than gut-wrenching surprise) was that it had an impressive, lustrous coat and a characteristically big brown muzzle. This bruin was a beautiful specimen, and by no means seemed a threat in the short time we eyed one another in disbelief.

Sensible bear-encounter protocol mandated that I quickly assure this keeper of the woods that I was a mere human and not worthy of a fight. Should I not do so, certainly the notorious "bluff charge" would result. This would require an attempt to stand my ground and resist the overwhelming urge to run.

Most all charges from both black and brown bears are bluff charges. They are sudden and sometimes ferocious advances toward a perceived threat to see how it will react in an attempt to determine the trespasser's intent. Such close encounters most always fall short of direct contact when the intruder holds fast or retreats slowly.

Worse outcomes, though seldom, have historically led to varying degrees of biting, more intensive mauling, and to human death, especially where a mother bear and her cubs or a bear near its cache are involved. This surprise encounter that was playing out before me was to be taken seriously.

As my twenty-plus years of knowledge and experience gained from mistakes made had taught me, I quickly raised my hands together to clap. Never did I consider the gun on my side as an option, for such encounters, while startling, should not result in harm if I did the right thing. My intent was to make noise and show movement that would identify me as a mere *Homo sapiens*.

The only manner in which to describe the next instant as I recount it is to say that the bear vanished. Though my hands never connected, the bruin did not turn around and retreat; it did not saunter off to one side into the undergrowth; the bear simply disappeared into the mist coming from the adjacent river. For a moment, I stood more in amazement at this phenomenon than with any anxiety of what the outcome could have been.

Now the stupid part becomes apparent. Casting all knowledge of safety in bear country aside and without any consideration of what I was really doing, I rushed toward the point at which I had just seen this beast depart. I intuitively did this as if to make some sense of its sudden disappearance. As I stood there, I realized that this move had been insane, but there was not a trace of the bear to be found.

There was not a sound of its mass crashing undergrowth in escape. There was not a clue that the bear had ever stood in the trail, with its cover of loose litter and damp, black soil. The slightest impact should have left some trace, but no prints, no pivoting claw marks—there was nothing!

I could not see very far down the trail toward the parking lot because of the encroaching evergreens, but I could see enough to know if the bear had retreated in that direction. Had the imposing figure plunged down the shallow bank to swim the river? Would I not have witnessed that, either?

His departing the trail opposite the river was not an option, not without noise or disturbance of the vegetation, for it was lush and dense. The black form was just too big and the terrain too unfavorable for it simply to have retreated into the brush, as bears often do when abruptly encountered (that is if they do not bluff charge first). It was simply gone, never to be seen by me again.

Walking on out and perplexed that there was no explanation for its whereabouts, only bewildered fascination, my thoughts turned to a second interesting phase of this event. I concluded that initially the bear might have been traveling toward the family when it smelled, heard, or saw them as they made their way to the parking lot. I suspect that the bear simply stepped into the undergrowth a short distance and, undetected, allowed them to pass. It was probably unaware that I was a distance behind them and heading out as well.

Processing all the information that the bear had at that point, it determined that the family was the only intruder. The bruin then made its way back onto the trail and proceeded in my direction assuming it was now alone. Not expecting to encounter another human, it was just as surprised to see me as I was to see it.

My lack of vigilance resulted from believing that all the scent, noise, and calamity of this family unit would have sent any creature scampering for cover. Both bear and man had blundered. I would only speculate that the bear left annoyed with the intrusions.

For me though, this ghost of the Resurrection River reaffirmed the mystique of nature and renewed my fascination with a bear's awesome prowess.

CHAPTER 5

Bears of the Appalachian Trail

Actually, we saw very few.

The legendary Appalachian Trail, completed in 1937 and commonly referred to as the AT, extends from the mountains of North Georgia all the way up the Southern Appalachian chain of mountains to the Northern Mountains of Maine. This is only if you call yourself a Southerner.

Those claiming home north of the Mason-Dixon Line explain its route in the reverse order, thus from Maine's Mt. Katahdin to Georgia's Springer Mountain. Either way, it extends for 2,175 miles along predominantly mountain crests of the most rugged countryside east of the Mississippi River.

The halfway point of the AT is found within Pine Grove Furnace State Park off Interstate 81, just north of where the states of Maryland, Pennsylvania, Virginia, and West Virginia converge. Completing the journey to Pine Grove from either direction is a significant accomplishment and milestone for those intent on completing the entire trail.

The AT makes its way through fourteen states and traverses two extraordinary national parks: Great Smoky Mountains along the state lines of North Carolina to the east and Tennessee to the west, and Shenandoah somewhat north of central Virginia.

It is not only defined by those individuals from all walks who tread upon it, the varied communities through which it passes, and the natural splendor that flourishes about it, but it also is identified by blaze markings. To assure the hiker that they are on the right path, over 300,000 of these 2" x 6" white-painted markings adorn trees, rocks, road crossings, and other visible structures, *even in the bottom of a canoe,* to direct those who hike the trail.

There is one infamous portion of the trail that crosses Maine's Kennebec River by canoe 152 miles south of Mt. Katahdin. Before entering the Hundred Mile Wilderness outside Monson, Maine, hikers are ferried across the dam-controlled river for their own safety.

Additionally, there are thirty regional trail clubs, comprised almost exclusively of volunteers, and multiple partnerships responsible for its care. While officially it comes under the protection of the Department of Interior's National Park Service, most hikers will never see a green uniform; it is mostly a self-policing entity, as well it should be.

The Appalachian Trail is an uninterrupted gateway to adventure, learning, and renewal that in addition to climbing mountains passes near and through farmlands, national forestland, small communities, and towns. It crosses rivers—lots of them—rural roads, major highways, and over and under interstates.

This tiny thread on a map extends the opportunity for personal solitude, physical challenge, and an immense education on natural history found no other place in the world. I have often expressed to college students eager to learn of its value that hiking the Appalachian Trail would provide the best education one ever could attain, far superior to that of a bachelors degree, but no one is hiring!

So, how many bears did we see as we journeyed from Georgia to Maine? Well, we did not see very many.

The reason is probably twofold. While hiking most of the trail, we had other folks with us, so the scent and noise was greater than had it just been the two of us. Also, we were covering considerable distance with each day's walk, and so we had less time to peruse the landscape than had we been moving at a slower pace and searching for bears.

I took my initial hike on the Appalachian Trail just after Christmas 1975 with three other friends, and together, we decided that we would hike the seventy-mile section through the Great Smokies. John Bilbrey, Lee Thompson, Terry Willard, and I set out to complete this awesome task in just six days.

Needless to say, *we were idiots!* And of course, being wintertime, we saw no bears. However, several years later, in the grip of winter, Kathy and I would encounter our first winter proof that they existed: an unmistakable bear track in the snow. This paw print was on a log, where no doubt the bear had awakened from its deep sleep (torpor), and relocated to another den site.

The four of us on this 1975 venture were *certified idiots* because:

#1 We had never backpacked even one day together.

#2 None of us had ever backpacked in the wintertime.

#3 We had never backpacked in the Smokies.

#4 None of us had a clue as to the tremendous undertaking a hike of seventy miles would be under wintertime conditions, with significant portions of the hike above five thousand feet in elevation and temperatures in the single digits above and below zero.

Nevertheless, we lived to tell the tale. At least Lee and I did, but he was not able to complete the entire route, bowing out with John and his chronic knee issue after just the second day and then rejoining me later near Newfound Gap. Terry would be plagued with issues of fitness and have to retreat homeward from the Gap where Lee and I reconnected.

Now, this is not to infer that these mortals were weaklings; far from it. They were incredible hikers and are valued friends to this day. All of us were ill-prepared. It was just a fluke that I was able to consistently hike the entire length and not succumb to fatigue, dehydration, hypothermia, or even death, as the wintertime conditions of freezing cold, ice, and snow were brutal and relentless.

Cubs of Standing Indian Mountain

My initial Field Biology offering involved hiking 113 miles on the trail in 1979, beginning fifty-one miles north of Springer at Unicoi Gap and eventually exiting at Fontana Dam. It was on this journey with eight aspiring biology students that I would encounter my first bear of the Appalachian Trail and hook-up with a new dog that would become the second love of my life.

I was in the lead, and the others were all strung out along the ridgeline a little beyond the high point of Standing Indian Mountain (just under 5,500 feet), a portion of North Carolina's Nantahala Wilderness. The AT makes its way slightly beneath its summit, and we were making our way along a grassy downhill slope.

Two cubs suddenly burst into sight just in front of me and bolted for a tree about thirty yards away. They let out a squeal that no doubt signaled to their mother that they were in trouble. That dog was close, but I had no idea where she had gone.

My immediate thought, though a novice at handling bear issues, was that the mother would pick up our scent—and worse, that of the dog—and race to investigate, taking drastic action in defense of her newborns. The fledging hikers in my care must also have sensed the danger, for without need of command they bunched-up tightly behind their queasy leader.

We had no idea of the mother bear's whereabouts, other than to be certain she was not too far from her young. No option availed but to quietly and hastily continue our walk northward on the trail. We hoped that she was not just ahead of our party, for encountering her would likely have been frightful.

My knowledge of bears at the time was minimal. I was confident that the mother bear would certainly charge, thus bolstering our exit from the area. Though it is rare for any bear to charge and injure hikers in a group, commonly thought of as "a bear-proof party," I did not know this at the time.

Distance began to separate us from the treed cubs as we marched in tight formation down the mountain and back into the cover of the trees beneath the summit. Our newfound canine friend soon joined us from the rear with no indication that she had processed the potential gravity of the moments before.

As days passed, her name evolved from "Appalachia" to just "AT." She was a mixed mutt whom we had found at a pull-off where the trail crossed Georgia's US Highway 76 at Dick's Creek Gap. We had endured rain for two miles into the journey from Unicoi Gap and stopped for lunch, spreading out our wet gear in the sunshine. It was then that we noted the dog slinking in the laurel.

She was a handsome, medium-sized dog of brown and black color, obviously with some German Shepherd bloodline. Nearby lay a trashcan lid upturned with remnants of dog food some charitable soul had left behind upon discovery of this waif.

She looked abandoned, a little scared, but eager for companionship from our group. There was no resisting the idea of allowing her to join us as we soon made our way back onto the trail after sharing our lunch scraps with her.

Now, I did not need a dog, and it seemed that no one else was inspired to take her home. Nonetheless, we jokingly repeated over the next thirteen days that if she stayed with us to Fontana Dam, someone would take her home. She did, so I did.

Our dog AT hiked more than nine hundred miles of the Appalachian Trail over the next fourteen years, with not only Kathy and me, but also on five additional Field Biology hiking trips, each time carrying her own pack. She completed all the trail from Dick's Creek to Pen Mar at the Maryland-Pennsylvania state line. This excluded the stint through the Smokies, because park regulations do not allow dogs on the trails.

We estimate that she probably hiked the nine hundred miles at least twice, for she would venture out, back and forth, but always return with an eagerness to be at our side. Adding to her repertoire, she traveled with me on college trips to the Outer Banks of North Carolina's coastline for about a dozen years before joining others of God's greatest creations in March 1994 at the age of sixteen. She truly was a remarkable companion, admired and adored by everyone who met her.

Thief in the Night

The area looked like the site of a plane crash! That bear had scattered the contents of the new Coleman Peak 1® pack all about the woods below our campsite.

Kathy took her first hike with me on the AT during the summer of 1980 while pursuing an engineering degree at the University of Tennessee in Knoxville. This was seven years before we were destined to marry.

On this second Roane State Field Biology offering, she enrolled to hike eighteen days on the trail, from the Smokies' eastern terminus of Davenport Gap to Roan Mountain State Park in upper East Tennessee. The most memorable recollection, second only to the belief that she would die from this initial grueling 137-mile adventure, would be experiencing her first bear.

It was early one morning at Little Laurel shelter, fifty-five miles into our northbound hike to Roan Mountain. We had crossed NC Highway 208/TN Highway 70 at Allen Gap and decided to press on five miles more beyond the crossing.

From a safety viewpoint, I thought it was a good idea to put some distance between a rural highway and our group. Throughout our travels over the entire length of the AT, we would camp away from rural roads and highways to reduce the possibility of locals harassing us in the middle of the night.

We made this prudent decision over the remaining decade of our hiking with six or more friends, though the group often included Gene Robbins, a career police officer, and Dick Lee, aka "Big 'Un." It could be just too much of a temptation for a few liquored-up good ol' boys to destroy a night's sleep and perhaps escalate into a more threatening situation.

In fall 2005, when Kathy and I completed the remaining 220 miles of the trail in Maine, we never camped near the trail. Often we would hike a ways perpendicular to it and pitch our tent, building a small fire at times, where no one would have detected our presence.

This also avoided the inevitable of having to relay our life history to other passersby, should we meet on the trail. It also provided a greater chance of privacy for the inevitable cold-water bath.

Beyond Allen Gap, the Little Laurel shelter provided sleeping space for only five occupants; being the "professor," I was privy to one of them. Several of my students had to pitch their tents behind the shelter. One of them was Charles, who had just purchased a Coleman Peak 1® pack, slightly used, but it was his joy.

I have always thought that Coleman® should never have engaged in the backpacking market, but rather perfected what they did best, making family-oriented camping gear.

Though they have made some innovative gear since the 1980s, and the Peak 1® experienced impressive sales and ratings, I never felt their packs ranked up there with those made by Kelty® or JanSport®. Besides, there was something cheap and weak-looking about the external resin frame. It just did not seem strong enough, compared to that made from aircraft aluminum found in JanSport® and Kelty® packs.

We knew there was the possibility of bears in the area because we had seen paw prints in the soft soil of the trail a ways from our evening's destination. Nonetheless, the only precaution that I was moved to take as leader of this group was to position all our packs up at the foot of our shelter's sleeping platform when we crawled into our bags.

Thinking back, I suppose my reasoning was that if the packs were close to us, along with AT (the dog!) bedded down under the wooden platform, a bear would not disturb them. Wrong!

More than once, she awakened us in the night, growling as if something was out front in the woods. But we never saw or heard anything, other than AT's growls. AT must have sensed it. Later we would learn that it had been a good-sized bear.

We never saw it, but these episodes created a sense of eeriness in the dark of night. We would sit up and shine our flashlights into the abyss before quickly fading back into slumber from another tiring day of hiking.

Up early the next morning, Charles came down for his pack to gather his belongings in preparation for breakfast. With no pack to be found, he was just certain that he had become the object of a college prank. There were always many on such college trips, and I delighted in being a contributor.

After a while, everyone became serious enough that I believed something else had taken his pack. We fanned out and began looking about the neighboring woods for the Peak®.

Just out of our view from the shelter's front side were the scattered remains of what had been Charles pack and our food. In my outdoor explorations, I have walked up on the remnants of a few tragic plane crash sites, and that is what this mayhem resembled.

Debris was splayed about, and every morsel of freeze-dried food had been removed from the Mountain House® foil pouches that he carried as his share of his group's rations. Obviously motivated by curiosity, every item Charles carried in his pack had been sampled, no doubt for food value, by sharp teeth. Even the cover from his trail guidebook was partially ripped off.

I felt sorry for Charles because his pack was torn to shreds, and he had been so proud of his purchase for this trip. Out came the dental floss, and the task of sewing it back together began so that he could again carry most of his gear. In time, we had licked our wounds, and we were on our way to Roan Mountain.

At the next shelter, we discovered in reading the trail journal customarily found at each location, that a problem bear had wreaked havoc on other unsuspecting campers in the region. A lesson learned. For the balance of our journey, we remained more vigilant and attentive to signs along the way.

Finally arriving at Roan Mountain State Park (a five-mile walk down the road from Hughes Gap), we pressed our sewing skills back into service. Just before reaching the endpoint of our journey, AT (again, the dog!) pushed through a barbed wire fence, ripping a two-inch gash just under her foreleg.

I carried suturing material, and we were able to repair the damage. Arriving back home, a trip to the vet affirmed our impressive trail skills.

Other Bears

Aside from repetitive hikes along the Appalachian Trail in the Smokies and Shenandoah, most of our bear encounters for the balance of the trail were unremarkable.

I recall watching a big, chubby bear cross fifty or so yards in front of Big 'Un and me just before the AT entered New Jersey from northern Pennsylvania.

With its head downturned, and paying little attention to us less a casual glance, it appeared to be on a mission and hastened out of sight. Dividing the distance of 229 miles across PA into two trips of a couple of miserable weeks each, our group of seven concluded that the bear was eager to get out of Pennsylvania.

Wayne Buchanan detested the rocky path through Pennsylvania so badly that he claimed to avoid even purchasing gasoline in the state as we made numerous highway trips north to complete the Trail.

His disdain prevailed until we entered New Hampshire. Pennsylvania sucked all right, with its uneven rock-strewn path over monotonous flat-line ridges, but it paled in comparison to the drudgery we would face in negotiating the White Mountains.

Every day's hike through Pennsylvania presented the same dread—struggling to remain upright and ending the day without blistered feet or twisted ankles. There were sections where we truly walked days without boot soles ever connecting with dirt.

There was another memorable bear that startled Wayne while fetching water in a stream at a backpacker site just before New Jersey's Sunfish Pond. The established camping site was complete with warning signs and storage devices to keep food away from bears that might visit in the night.

After we had set up our tents and secured our gear, Wayne ventured down to the neighboring stream and encountered a bear in the brown tannic water common to the area. I can remember that he rejoined us wide-eyed and excited from the confrontation but grateful that he returned to camp unscathed.

Once we made it to New Hampshire, we reflected back on Pennsylvania with greater kindness. These Yanks had been folksy and hospitable, though they sometimes struggled with our Southern dialect. Had we tarried we would have taught them to talk right!

New Hampshire's massive boulders and scree fields, a lack of any sense of a trail through some sections, and precipitous vertical ascents and descents where death loomed should one fall plagued us from New Hampshire into Maine until summiting Mt. Katahdin.

We would notice only one set of bear prints in the deep forest of Maine, several miles south of Baxter State Park. I remember well that we were climbing up a ridge through a tight, scratchy gauntlet of evergreens when I looked down at the unmistakable paw print of a bear in the black soil. This was not surprising, because Maine's Department of Inland Fisheries and Wildlife estimates the state's bear population to be in excess of 23,000.

Guided by instinct, bears commonly retreat to trees when they sense danger. So I have often pondered: we did not see that many bears on the AT, but how many saw us?

CHAPTER 6

TRAPPED

*The District Ranger radioed back almost immediately—I
told Kathy that she had a job to do.*

*There were many of these wild hog traps dispersed
throughout the park. Our participants always found them
to be of interest when we pointed one out. Never had we
expected to find one occupied with what we saw late that
afternoon.*

Don had been to Spence Field in the Smokies before, but this
August weekend, he had chosen to go with us through an
offering of the Smoky Mountain Field School called "Big Game
Observation."

This participant was a local surgeon about my age, and he had
a younger girlfriend who was lesser in years, like Kathy's and my
age span. Of greater interest, he knew where there was a hog trap

opposite the shelter on the western slope of the ridge. We did not know of this one, and it would prove to be an intriguing find.

In the 1980s, it seemed that Russell and Spence Fields were the places to go to see bears in the summer, and that has not changed much. The attraction is more than these high-altitude meadows where patches of heath and other assorted shrubs threaten to swallow them up.

Prior to the park's establishment in 1934, in the latter 1800s and early 1900s, these balds were grazing grounds for livestock of pioneer settlers in the Cades Cove area below. How these high mountaintops established themselves as open meadows with scant trees is still a mystery and long debated.

Today, the Park Service, through seasonal maintenance efforts, keeps some of them cleared as they appeared before the turn of the century. Among these are Andrews and Gregory balds. More than twenty varieties of azaleas flourish on Gregory Bald, and their floral display makes the six-mile hike out of Chestnut Flat worth the effort on a sultry, late June day when they are at their peak.

Serviceberry trees growing on Russell and Spence balds seemed to the two of us to attract a disproportionately higher number of bears than other meadows. The bruins favored them to feast upon in preparation for torpor, or prolonged sleep, in the winter months to come. White oak acorns, a major player in the fall mast crop, became their favorite food source as fall approached later.

The word "hibernation" is often used loosely and erroneously to describe a phase in the black bear's seasonal lifecycle, just like the word "buffalo" is mistakenly used to identify bison found in the western plains. Buffalo are not native to North America, though many a green uniform will refer to our shaggy bison as such when they relate to us the natural history features of national parks.

"Although popularly said to hibernate, black, grizzly, and female polar bears do not. Instead, they enter a deep winter sleep from which they easily arouse. They do not enter extreme hibernation.

The bears do not eat, drink, urinate, or defecate. Females give birth to and nurse young during this sleep and they maintain a metabolism that is near normal." (Robert Leo Smith and Thomas M. Smith)

They seek out hollowed trees and wedge themselves inside, where the surrounding wood and the bear's heavy fat layer from fall gorging provide a good insulation from winter's fury. While in such cramped quarters for several months, there is no significant atrophy of muscle tissue, but the fat reserve diminishes by springtime.

A fall mast failure can lead to undernourished bears entering the den site and never reappearing in the spring. The fall hard mast favorite is the white oak acorn, while the earlier soft mast harvest was certain to include various heath berries—blueberries and huckleberries, as well as blackberries, serviceberries, and wild strawberries.

During this deep sleep when they do not defecate, they form a fecal plug that is expelled in the early weeks of springtime. I have often thought that I would not want to be too close when that "plug" was expelled from an awakening bear eager to seek relief and thus be able to feed ravenously on early vegetation.

They do not eat during this period of dormancy; besides, there would little of nutritional value to feed upon during the winter months. However, they may abandon an initial den site for another location if disturbed. We have not encountered bears during our winter forays, but we have found tracks in the snow affirming this wanderlust.

A prolonged winter or a dry spring can be disastrous to emerging bears, especially those with young cubs. Life is hard enough for the young. Often, mortality is over fifty percent of those born, and bears only give birth every two years.

Two cubs born to the mother is expected; three is infrequent; and we have observed female bears with four alongside. These naked, blind blobs weigh about a pound at birth, and instinct quickly drives them to a nipple for rich nourishment or else they perish.

The mother and her young stay close to the den site early in the spring, and she is very protective of them. In bear country, it is not a prudent thing to go about a wildflower walk in late March or early April focused solely toward the ground. Rather, look outward frequently in anticipation that a young bear family might be foraging for breakfast.

During our August trips to the high-elevation balds that we made in the 1980s, it was common to experience several bear-with-cub sightings. By late summer, cubs had put on weight and begun to venture out of their mother's sight, investigating whatever piqued their interest. This was not limited to food, such as blueberries, huckleberries, or serviceberries, but might also include a neglected backpack.

Encountering an unsuspecting pair of cubs is almost certain to initiate a hectic and frightful squeal, eliciting a charging mother bear in defense of whatever startled her progeny. Mother bears are fearless when protecting their cubs. We have seen average female grizzlies in Alaska take on much larger males to defend their young, thus passing along their genes, as instinct mandates.

Our goal on this weekend overnighter was to place our participants in an area where we were likely to see bear activity, along with the possibility of seeing a white-tail or two, and possibly a wild hog. These feral pigs are often called boar in the mountains of East Tennessee and Western North Carolina.

Actually, the word "boar" refers to a male bear or hog, so wild hog is the preferred term. A turkey would also be nice to see, but they were less frequent at that time than on future trips to this same area twenty years hence. Elk would be reintroduced to the eastern end of the park in early 2000 to become the fifth big game animal inhabiting the Smokies.

Upon laboring upward in our five-mile journey from the Cades Cove area, we would settle in at the backcountry shelter and hope for an animal visit as dusk approached. Our early afternoon arrival would encompass arranging our sleeping bags on lumpy wire bunks and gathering water from the pipe extending from the bank's spring down the hill at the back of the shelter.

While at the water source, Kathy and I would take a quick bath by filling a cook pot or two with the icy water, soaping down, and hastily rinsing off in the neighboring woods before donning clean clothes for the evening.

We had always enjoyed being out in the wilderness. However, without reservation of becoming sweaty and nasty to reach some remote destination, we detested the thought of crawling in a sleeping bag wet and smelly from a day's hike. Besides, late evening and early morning would provide the best opportunity to witness bears feeding among the serviceberries.

As we made our nest for the evening and rested a bit, members of our group would venture about in curiosity and in need of a nature break. Some would report back with interesting discoveries, such as a colorful patch of cardinal flower or some unusual shape of scat that begged to be identified by the leaders. Participants, too, had always been good on such trips to assist with chores for the evening, such as hauling water or gathering firewood.

Fires, while a much-favored part of the outdoor camping experience, were often discouraged because of the impact that decades of them have had on the vegetation from careless gatherers. Some thought nothing about bringing down green wood from standing understory trees found around the shelters. Back then and today, fires are restricted to established shelter and tent sites and must be confined to metal enclosures.

Most shelter fireplaces have even been closed off in recent years to eliminate their use and send the fire-builders outside to the fire rings. Besides, most of the wood, laurel, and yellow birch gathered at these five-thousand-foot elevations produced little warmth, but lots of smoke. That is, if one could find wood that was dry in an area that frequently received twice as much annual rainfall as the forty-five inches recorded in the lower elevations.

Around mid-afternoon, Don informed me of the whereabouts of a wild hog trap set by the Park Service to catch an unwary "pig." It seemed that he and his new friend had ventured over the hillside and stumbled onto it. It was out of sight of the short section of the Appalachian Trail that all of us had walked to make our connection with the side trail leading down to the shelter. While Kathy and I knew the locations of several of these "wire boxes," we were not aware of this one so near the shelter.

There are literally dozens of these traps, each similar to a small refrigerator and weighing about eighty pounds, located throughout the park. Most traps are unset during much of the year, but during the warm seasonal trapping period, many are baited with corn in hopes of attracting a catch. A sow with several piglets would be *a bonus.*

Wild hogs are considered exotic or foreign to the park, and evidence of them is undisputed along many trails and high-elevation hillsides. They put their snouts to the ground and furrow up long trenches of the park's rich soil in search of anything edible, leaving behind a path of destruction and opportunity for erosion.

The wild hog was introduced into the southern Appalachians around 1912, when George Moore set out to establish a private hunting preserve in western North Carolina, where the Joyce Kilmer Memorial Forest is located today. The hunting lodge was sold in time to his manager, Cotton McGuire, and fell into financial ruin soon afterward. While it seemed like a clever idea for the period, the distance and difficulty in reaching the lodge proved too much of a deterrent for wealthy would-be guests.

Not only were wild hogs brought to the high mountain enclosure, but also bison, elk, and grizzly bears. Over time, most were either killed by locals or died from lack of suitable habitat.

Some hogs escaped and expanded their range into the neighboring forest. There they mated with domestic swine that ranged freely on government land and gave rise to the feral pigs seen today.

Since the mid-1960s, the Park Service has had an ongoing hog eradication program in place to remove as many of them as possible from the backcountry. Seasonal rangers hunt at night, walking trails in areas where hogs are known to frequent. Additionally, the dozens of traps located throughout the park are used to target specific regions where these aliens thrive.

Hogs and piglets caught in traps are shot and disposed of near the location of the trap. At best, it is a difficult task to locate and shoot them at night, even with sophisticated weapons, or passively capture and destroy them, due to their keen senses and elusive behavior. Their sheer numbers and ability to breed and produce offspring any time of the year translates to a perpetual expense and problem for park managers.

Traps are constructed of woven wire shaped into a rectangular box about six feet long and three feet square. Heavy metal rods comprise their infrastructure, and a sliding trap door completes the device.

At the top is a "coon hole" that allows the escape of smaller game that fall for the enticement of the grain placed on the floor. Park biologist Bill Stiver once told me of a bobcat that became trapped simultaneously with a frantic deer. The bobcat lost.

Any animal venturing into a live trap might trigger the simple, pegged trip-line set amidst the corn kernels on the floor. Once the line is tripped, the metal door is released and it slides quickly from its upward support to close off the entrance. Trapped animals do not have the ability to raise the door, although it slides freely by human hand within its frame. The floor is laced with the same type of wire that comprises the sidewalls and ceiling to prevent an animal from digging itself free when trapped.

Don was excited about finding the trap, and our interest heightened because we could use it for "show and tell." We always looked forward to discovering something new and unique that would be of interest to our participants and affirm the value of our leadership. Therefore, Kathy and I ventured over the hill with Don and his friend and disappeared into the woods. In approaching his "find," we soon realized that it had an occupant. It is dark and hairy, but surprisingly it was not a hog. It was a *bear,* and a very agitated bear at that!

Upon sensing these interlopers, the bear went berserk, thrashing about as if it were going to rupture the rather secure prison cell that had held it captive. Realizing that these traps were substantial but not built to withstand the forceful antics of a frustrated bear, we quickly retreated in the direction from which we had come to evaluate what to do about this discovery.

We reasoned that it was best not to disturb the bear further, believing that it might cause harm to itself or, more alarming, break out and harm us. Kathy and I also decided to relay this discovery back to the park communication center by the radio that we carried as VIPs (Volunteers in the Park).

Because it is the duty of park employees to interact with the public, park visitors easily overhear broadcasts from radios carried by rangers. Realizing this, we made the decision to communicate our information to "Como" or "700" (the central communications center located in the bowels of the park headquarters building outside of Gatlinburg) late in the evening.

Many of those radios would be at rest in their recharging cradles, and the bulk of park visitors would be enjoying taffy or fudge in nearby stores. To elicit a run on the area and its bear by throngs of curiosity seekers would not be prudent and could prove to be dangerous to both man and our newfound beast.

As our day progressed from dinner and animal watching in the meadow nearby to late evening, we made radio contact with "700." Our information was acknowledged with appreciation but without emotion, as bear issues are no surprise to those who wear the uniform.

Comfortable that we had done the right thing by retreating from the stressed bruin and reporting its status to the park, we expected nothing more than a peaceful evening with our group. However, within minutes of our transmission, a call came back to us from the Cades Cove district ranger.

When we received the call, with its request that we release the bear, Kathy was not in sight. Somewhat surprised and somewhat excited in our fledgling knowledge of bears, I eagerly summoned my companion from the shelter and related *that she now had a job to do!*

As the forthcoming task began to gel within our minds, we decided to wait until morning, when the bear would have had time to adjust to its predicament and we would be fresh, since we'd had a hard hike the day before. While a night in a shelter generally provided only a visit by one or more skunks in search of food, if it were a clear night, it would bring forth a brilliant canopy of stars with no interference from humanity's lighted comforts. Secure behind the shelter's bear fence, everyone settled in for a much-deserved sleep, despite the discomfort afforded by the uneven sleeping surfaces.

Waking to a beautiful morning and breakfast in one of the park's special places, we began to pack and make plans for a mid-morning hike back up the hill, retracing our steps of the day before to where the shelter side trail rejoined the AT. Our plan was to place everyone a safe distance from the trap, where they could see the release but not be at risk should the bear do something threatening upon attaining its freedom.

In addition, we did not want to add further chaos to an already over-stressed animal. Kathy would stay back with the group, and it would be my job to pull the rope, raise the door, and thus release the bear.

As a biologist only out of graduate school ten or so years, I had had no direct experience with this procedure, but I was familiar with the intent: to free the bear unharmed and avoid its wrath. It astonished me that the park would encourage us to free the bear, given their bureaucratic propensities and the possible legal implications should something go awry and harm come to someone.

Nonetheless, we felt appreciated and respected to be given this opportunity. After all, we carried a park radio and both had green hats with the Park Service emblem attached to them. We were VIPs!

VIPs could also stand for "Very Ignorant People" when it came to taking the bait and releasing a bear from a trap designed for hogs. Considering how cautious the Park Service is in every facet of its management policy today, park managers reading of this event will gasp at the thought of the scenarios that could have resulted in a mishap. One could just imagine the thick manual on risk management that would be generated from this hapless undertaking.

Excitement grew among the onlookers as I neared the trap from behind. While certainly this was a first among my many outdoor experiences, I did not consider it much of a challenge. I approached the site quietly and slowly. The imprisoned bear seemed leery of me but okay with my intrusion into the space surrounding the trap.

This wire fortress had been positioned next to a medium-sized tree and below a large, overhanging branch. The limb would allow me to position myself over the cage without obstructing the doorway or being on ground level when the bear gained its freedom. My plan was to hoist myself up over the top's coon hole and tug on the rope, hopefully raising the door and releasing the bear.

This was all theory at this point, of course. I knew enough from wildlife courses that I should illustrate to that bear that I was in charge of the situation, thus my dogwood hiking stick accompanied me as I lifted myself above the enclosure.

The idea that I had, which I had seen in taped videos of other bear releases, was to thrash the side of the trap with the stick as the bear escaped. This aggressive behavior was to make the bear feel threatened enough to move away, with no thought of turning on me.

I was looking good to the group, I thought. Kathy must be proud, as I seemed to approach this beast with no sign of trepidation, as if I were an old hand at coping with nature's fiercest creatures.

I appeared calm so I would not upset the bear as I assumed my final position hanging onto the bent tree limb directly over him. This was all going too well. My adrenaline level soared when the bear decided that some attempt must be made to shift the experience from the ordinary to a state of stark terror!

Without a blink, the bear flipped upside-down and locked all four feet onto the top of the cage from within as he lunged with an open-mouth to within inches of my face.

Of course, there was the trap's metal fencing between the bear's teeth and my fleshy frame, but such reasoning was not a part of this moment. I could smell his awful breath.

In sheer fright, I reeled backward at the same time the crowd gasped and the bear went into a growling oratory that deafened me. It was a "pants-peeing" moment if ever there was one, but time and space did not permit a face-saving retreat.

After what seemed an eternity but was actually mere seconds, I am certain, he calmed down a bit. As I attempted to regain my composure, the bear suddenly developed interest in the door that was slightly elevated above ground, thanks to my my flinching grasp on the release rope.

With the bear's focus on escape rather than on the ruination of his savior, I raised the door completely and frantically thrashed my stick on the side of the trap. The bear hurled itself through the opening and gained its freedom. A second gasp of awe came from my audience as I collapsed onto the frame in disbelief but relieved.

As if jettisoned from its captive state, the bear exploded out of the cage and bolted about forty feet from the trap's entrance. The bear came to rest on its haunches and looked back at what had held it imprisoned for the night. It must have been rather amusing to see me collapsed atop the cage with my stick still in hand and a crowd of humans staring back in astonishment.

Quickly, he retreated deeper into the woods and disappeared from view. I crawled back down from the trap, ignored my desire to go limp, and rejoined our group as if such tasks were a normal part of my day. For after all, I was their leader on this brief expedition. I was a VIP!

Never mind that this experience was the first for me; I was confident that was the first and likely the last of such escapades for the bewildered bear.

CHAPTER 7

Sassy "Teenager"

That bear wanted to pick a fight, and we were not sure what would save us.

With every cycle, she inhaled and exhaled in a low, guttural rattle. While I do not recall even a hint of her scent, as is often said to be observed in some encounters, I noted that even her dark lips had a wet, saliva-laden, glossy glow. We were that close.

The spot where we were positioned provided no route of escape should a bear decide to come closer for inspection, and there she stood—a mother bear with two large year-old cubs.

On this August 1995 trip to Alaska's Kodiak Island, I flew to the village of Old Harbor and met up with Matt Reid and Steve Gehman. We were to travel by small plane to Karluk Lake and join Scott Shelton at the cabins on Camp Island. Then we were to raft across the lake to the main body of Kodiak and watch bears as they fished the Thumb River.

Our intent was to gain information about the bruins and assist Kodiak's native corporation in exploring opportunities for ecotourism. I avoided using that buzzword because it gave (and still does) the illusion of aging hippies exploiting nature for profit while spewing out warm-fuzzies to gain grace among gullible, well-heeled donors.

Ecotourism to Old Harbor village meant sharing the plentiful natural resources of the region to bolster the economy without sacrificing the landscape and its treasures. Local residents had more respect for their holdings than naively to encourage hordes of yapping tourists clad in golf shirts and plaid shorts and embracing video cameras to besiege their community for a few needed bucks.

We took our usual route by raft from Camp Island across the lake to the mainland of Kodiak and waded ashore. Each person on board then would splash into the surf in their knee-high Tufs while another steadied the raft.

Afterward, Scott would ease the boat farther out from the bank to discourage a bear he called "Olga" and her two sizeable cubs from ravaging its contents while we were observing others of her breed from the bench. This technique seemed to work, even though these curious and massive brown bears were excellent swimmers.

The bench was a rectangular wooden platform about ten by fifteen feet. It was positioned above the river so observers could watch bears feeding below without upsetting the bear's routine. The bench provided no form of safety itself—nothing but good judgment separated man and the beasts that fed below it.

In our short walk to the bench, we passed only a few snoozing bruin as we made our way through the waist-high undergrowth onto the embankment where the platform was located. Snoozing, yes, but always alert to any human intrusion that might require discipline should their routine be out of the ordinary.

In my observations over the years, and it has been shared by others, bears when disturbed are a forgiving lot if allowed to save face. Generally, they are not looking for conflict with humans and often yield through avoidance behavior. Upon encountering a hiker, such behavior might simply involve scampering off to a trailside to a creek for a drink, and thus not having to deal with the intrusion.

To the hiker, this might be interpreted as the bear's reaction out of fear. However, in all likelihood it was simply the bear's way of avoiding the expenditure of energy involved in a bluff charge and therefore politely allowing the two-legger to pass unscathed.

Our journey so far had not been particularly remarkable. We knew to stay on the established path and to not do anything that might be perceived as a threat. It was exhilarating to walk among these lethargic giants.

I always felt relieved (and I could sense that everyone else did, too) when finally we had passed through the gauntlet and were on the bench a few hundred feet ahead. Somehow, the unquestioned power of the 12-gauge shotgun that we carried seemed insignificant when compared to the enormous mass of a brown bear.

While the others within our group conversed about bears (of course), I was always eager to set up my tripod and camera. I knew that visits to Kodiak and opportunities to be so close to these bears would likely be few.

This had been a treasured experience for me, being in the presence of such an abundance of nature's finest creatures. Growing up in the hills of East Tennessee, where the only animals comparable in size were the Santa Gertrudis cattle that we raised on our small farm, being among these bears was a true adventure.

As they came to feed within our view, some bears were obvious repeat visitors, distinguished by scars or particular markings that separated them from the balance. Others would be seen as newbies to the area, perhaps just learning of the riches that the waters of the Thumb River produced. Some bears came from miles away to join this summer feeding frenzy, which would only last a few weeks.

Soon, Kodiak's interior would be draped in white, and cold would prevail for months until a new spring arrived. Because of the prevailing warmer coastal winds, some of these bears never experienced the need to enter true hibernation. They would wander about in the months before spring returned and scavenge on whatever food source was found for the taking.

I never felt that we became complacent during the hours spent here. Looking back, it is difficult to imagine that I had ever been anything but in a constant adrenalin rush to be among these bears as they made their living on fresh Pacific salmon.

What I was seeing firsthand, the masses back home experienced only through television specials. Such TV "documentaries" were predominantly tainted with hype and hysteria, and were presented through the eyes of daffy photojournalists, many out of big cities and most of whom had no training in natural history. Today it seems to have only gotten worse, as they feel a need to entertain and threaten us 24/7 with the unthinkable.

Our observation platform had indeed been carefully located by our native hosts to allow for good visibility of the river and the area through which we made our daily approach. We also had a distant view of Camp Island about a mile away. From it, we could follow the Thumb River's meandering from our left to its endpoint into Karluk Lake. This gave us two hundred yards or so of relatively open viewing from left to right.

Occasionally, we would take note of the buzz overhead generated from the miniature plane operated by the US Fish and Wildlife Service in the relentless acquisition of data about many of these same bears. This had to have been the smallest plane that I had ever seen.

I would not have felt safe flying over such rugged environment in this contraption, given its fragile appearance. Looking upward, I could imagine some local taking it out as an alien craft if it had been circling back home. Its uniqueness certainly would have made our local paper, alongside pictures of the largest tomato gathered over summer or the biggest copperhead encountered.

In the flight approach to Old Harbor from the town of Kodiak, there was a grim reminder of the consequences of air travel in this region. Atop a mountain, just short of the gravel runway, was the upside-down wreckage of a small plane. Every recurring thought I had of that plane made me consider lightening my gear each time I flew into Old Harbor.

Sometime into morning, after we had enjoyed observing several bears, we noticed one pudgy female in the distant waist-high vegetation behind us. She appeared to be making her way in our direction with two rather portly but handsome cubs, definitely last year's crop—stately teenagers, if you will.

At first glance, she was intriguing, for she would rise up on her hind feet periodically and carefully gaze over the green landscape. She did this as if to scan for anything that might need further inspection before dropping once more to continue her travel toward our position.

Her cubs ventured out independently, pursuing whatever piqued their senses. Each one drifted away as if to chase a scent or inspect a blade of vegetation that aroused their curiosity. They would always return, knowing that a scolding would be forthcoming should they not cooperate in this joint venture of purposeful travel.

Bears often stand on their hind feet, directing all senses forward, as this stance enables them to best perceive any threats that might be lurking ahead. Any prolific reader of outdoor hunting magazines has seen countless slick covers depicting hunters attempting that frantic shot to kill a standing bear at close range.

While any bear appears more threatening and bigger than life in such a pose, especially when up close, such posture is not considered aggressive by those knowledgeable of bear behavior. The animals simply do this to get a better idea of what lies ahead.

The female made her way toward us, while the two cubs continued to sporadically and independently move about in opposing directions, investigating various things of interest. These teens seemed more interested in play and exploring the tussocks than in their mother's attempt to determine what lay ahead for them at the bench.

As they came within about fifty yards of our position, their proximity caused us to focus on their likely intentions. While occasional glances from the mother bear leading her cubs did not indicate any interest in us, the route they were taking would deliver them to our location if they continued.

We watched other bears catch salmon in the river below us, while more frequently glancing in the direction of the approaching trio. As the span between this bear family and the bench continued to shorten, it was clear that they were making their way to us.

Because they were now too close to the only path back to the raft, a retreat along the trail that had brought us here was not an option. Instead, we now found ourselves facing this family with the steep drop into the Thumb River behind us. This now had escalated into *a worrisome situation.*

I became more uncomfortable as they neared within thirty or so feet of our position. That feeling was not abated at all by the tension that I could feel from the others in my group. Every eye among us was now opened widely in the bear family's direction and gave no attention to the browns feeding on the Thumb below.

Attempting to estimate a bear's weight is a guess at best, even among much more experienced observers than I, but this was a sizeable family unit. I would venture that she weighed well over four hundred pounds and each cub more than half of that.

While she was light brown in color with no distinguishable markings, each of her tan offspring sported a white band of fur around its neck. This noticeable ring of color, or "necklace," was common among young bears. It generally would fade in time as the sub-adults acquired the lush uniform coat of a maturing brown bear.

There are three bear species common to North America. They are the black bear, which has the greatest range distribution, extending throughout many of the forty-eight states, Alaska, and Canada; the polar bear, which is generally limited to the upper regions of the Arctic; and the brown, or grizzly, bear. While the latter is found west of the Mississippi River and restricted mostly to the Yellowstone ecosystem, it is found in abundance throughout much of Alaska and Canada to the north.

Historically, the brown bear and grizzly bear were classified as two separate species, and the issue is still debated globally. I have a 1960s *Outdoor Life* coffee table book that supports the species' separation—the brown bear is noted as *Ursus gyas,* and the grizzly bear as *Ursus horribilis.*

Readers my age (sixty-two) should well remember as youngsters cajoling their parents into returning the magazine's accompanying postcard ("postage paid," back then), thereby joining a monthly outdoor book club. Unfortunately, my insistence on receiving free books cleverly offered as an enticement for the reader to purchase others obligated my mother to write multiple letters, eventually halting the barrage of "pay or return" selections.

Today, though considered separate species, DNA research supports the close relationship between browns and grizzlies. The coastal bears, such as those inhabiting Kodiak Island, are generally called "brown bears." Land-locked bears, such as those found within Yellowstone National Park, are referred to as "grizzlies."

Like their black bear relatives, brown bears and grizzly bears are primarily opportunistic carnivores, feeding mostly on vegetation but seldom passing on the chance acquisition of carrion or vulnerable live game. Often, brown bears live in a habitat ripe with fishing opportunities, and thus food sources rich in fat and protein, so they attain greater size than their more diminutive relatives do. No doubt, genetics play a vital role here also.

In the Lower Forty-Eight, grizzlies are mostly scattered within the Greater Yellowstone Ecosystem of the West, where their habitat overlaps with that of black bears. A cinnamon phase, or "more brown than black," black bear of the West might be mistaken to the untrained observer for a grizzly. Black bears found east of the Mississippi are always black, but as a biologist, I learned long ago to never say never.

No doubt, some idiot "east of the river" might release a grizzly into the wild that had been raised in their basement until it proved to be too unmanageable. Such a release would shortly set off a wave of unmatched hysteria until the truth was established. Kim Delozier, career park biologist for Great Smoky Mountains National Park, once told me that every animal imaginable had been dumped in the park, from peacocks to alligators.

Further, I always found it amusing that one difference between a black bear and a grizzly bear often cited in authoritative literature is the grizzly's "dished-in face." The close proximity required for most individuals to take note of this characteristic would be tantamount to that of observing the sensory pit between the eye and nostril of a pit viper. What sane individual would dare get close enough to discern such an appointment on a bear's face?

Grizzlies are repeatedly written up as being more aggressive than black bears, but I squirm with discomfort at that label. I am more at ease explaining that grizzlies are less forgiving upon encounter.

In addition, it is important to note that grizzlies are thought to have evolved on the plains, and black bears are said to have evolved in the forests. Growing up with no place to hide for the griz, no doubt, has molded over generations a "retreat is not an option" mentality, while evolving in the woodland offered multiple opportunities for escape from potential threats for the black bear.

Perhaps the reason that most backcountry explorers never see a black bear is that they have sensed the intruder's presence first and withdrawn to the trees. Having said this, though I have often looked upward in my countless wanderings and forced marches, I have seldom encountered a bear in a tree.

Generally, serious birders with their heads turned upward in their constant pursuit to add to the "life list" are more likely to see bears in trees. Most hikers I know stay focused on the trail before them in fear of stumbling headfirst to the ground with a loaded pack. Kathy and I have hiked many miles on the Appalachian Trail where we were so focused on staying upright that a trailside elephant might have escaped our view.

It is generally agreed upon that brown bears and grizzlies do not climb trees because of their size and an absence of suitable curvature in their claws. Black bears are often smaller and have shorter but much more curved claws, making them exceptional climbers. Nonetheless, I have witnessed more than one sizeable brown bear climb a tree in my Alaskan experiences.

There also is the joke, "How does one distinguish a black bear from a griz if you climb a tree?" The answer: "A black bear comes up after you, and the griz just knocks the tree down." However, documented accounts substantiate that both black bears and grizzlies have pulled humans down from trees upon provocation.

As advice to the individual traveling out West or to Alaska, I always state the necessity of respecting every bear as if it were a grizzly and giving it a wide berth. Avoidance of encounters is the best safety measure when sharing the same wilderness with bears, whether armed with a firearm or not. No caliber of firearm or experience using it can replace the advantage of good judgment and prevention when it comes to a hostile chance encounter.

Most often, the worst scenario in a confrontation with a black bear is an intense yet harmless bluff charge, and the ensuing requirement to reclaim one's composure and dignity after moments of rapid heart palpitations finally ease. A close encounter with a grizzly, especially one with "cubs-of-the-year," quite often leads to mauling or worse for the careless adventurer.

There does not seem to be a stronger signal that travels across the bruin's cerebral synapses than to protect its offspring at any risk, and thus to pass along its genes to the next generation. This can prove fatal to an unsuspecting intruder.

At the bench on Kodiak, none of us paid the slightest attention to the other members of our party, as we stood erect in our pose, now totally cemented upon the approaching threesome. In her prowess and beauty, the female eased up to within ten or twelve feet of our position as we froze in place, not knowing how this would play out.

She was not direct in her approach but was undoubtedly confident that we would be no match for her should a violent contact follow. That impressive 12-guage that we had brought along as protocol mandated seemed a pitifully unlikely deterrent to such force as she was capable of delivering if she chose to charge and attack us.

With her nose turned upward and her eyes fixed on us, she surveyed for an instant any possibility of a threat to herself or her accompanying progeny. We were close enough that I could see her nostrils expanding and relaxing with each breath she took.

With every cycle, she inhaled and exhaled in a low guttural rattle. While I do not recall even a hint of her scent, as is often said to be observed in some encounters, I noted that even her dark lips had a wet, saliva-laden, glossy glow that was discernable. We were that close.

After sampling the air with her massive snout for any signs of concern, she quickly seemed to lose interest in us. There was no huffing or chomping of teeth, as these mannerisms would have certainly indicated disdain for our party and elevated the fear for our safety.

Perhaps supported by generations of instinct and a few prior human dealings, she concluded that we were mere mortals of no obvious food value or particular significance. As precariously as she had approached us, she sauntered to our left away from the platform and disappeared into the lush vegetation.

Her massive frame was in harmony with each of her sizeable paws as they quietly carried her away. Her short, thick tuft of a tail gave no indication of emotion or concern as surely would be noted in a member of the dog family, a fox or coyote.

The two cubs, however, now presented a more daunting concern, as the larger of the two hastily made its way closer toward us and assumed the female's previous position. The sinister demeanor of this cub caused me to reflect back over my fifty-plus years. There was no doubt that he was looking for trouble, and I considered that this could be the last opportunity to relish my earthly appointment. Many times since, I simply have recounted that moment as a stare-down with a sassy teenager.

I can remember thinking of cartoons from my youth where a mischievous, freckle-faced boy was illustrated wearing a propeller cap above an impish face while carrying out a prank. The cub peered at us through dark eyes with a look of disdain, and for a moment, seemed to dare us to engage. He wanted to fight!

I have pilot friends who refer to flying as "hours of boredom interrupted by moments of stark terror." Boredom had sometimes overtaken us here after hours of repetitive bear sightings, but this was a moment of *stark terror.*

The nearby sibling never expressed interest but simply grunted, urging his kin to spare us the embarrassment of a defeat as he disappeared into the tall grasses and joined his mother. The moment was tense as this delinquent cub before us huffed a bit and retreated a few feet sideways, then gazed back as if to say, "I could have ..."

No doubt to further show his prowess and assure favor with his peer, he collapsed on his front legs and buried his massive head in the ground-level vegetation. From side to side, he vigorously rotated his head, sending up blades of tall grass and dirt as he snorted and blew in defiance of us.

This behavior went on for several seconds. All of us remained rigid in our stance. Then I recalled that the spot where the cub was so involved was where each of us had repeatedly stepped off the earthen mound to relieve ourselves when nature called over the course of our long day observing bears. He was flailing about in our urine!

Like a euphoric dog rolling on the carcass of a beached dead fish, this rebellious teen rebuked our mere existence through this act. He huffed and snorted repeatedly, and then departed with the other members of his disinterested family unit as if the scent from our presence had fouled all of Kodiak.

CHAPTER 8

Bathing with Bertha

*"Because you are a man, you did not listen.
I told you to watch for bears!"*

*Finally, she came back up the hill to where I was waiting.
There was a look on her face as if someone must have walked
up on her from the trail below. Kathy had been stripped-
down to her flip-flops, washing off trail grime a ways from
the stream. Bending over to refill her pot of water and
looking backward, she had been surprised, all right.*

Often quoted outdoor clothing commercial says, "It's not nice to fool Mother Nature." It is also "not nice to name bears," according to our friend and Smokies biologist Kim Delozier.

Kim's National Park Service title is sometimes noted in the local papers as "Wildlife Technician." The word "technician" does not do justice to his training and vast knowledge, accumulated over decades of field experiences within one of the country's finest parks.

The park is a better place due to Kim's dedication and significant contributions to the understanding of wildlife management within this diverse habitat.

In the latter years of my college career, I was privileged to teach a weeklong field biology class during the spring and summer intersession. Traveling in a fifteen-passenger van with twelve carefully screened students, we would camp in diverse areas of the park. For a reasonable fee, the institution even provided the meals, plus cooking and camping gear.

Prior to the course, I would schedule rangers with various backgrounds and in different roles to share their viewpoints on their jobs and park issues. This was a tremendous learning opportunity for wanna-be wildlife majors How much better could it get than to hear it from a green uniform already doing the job for which you were preparing?

I often gleaned from the rangers insightful tidbits to share with participants on other ventures that I led within the region. A visit to the park's small wildlife office behind the historic gray headquarters building was always interesting.

I could also count on Kim's respected coworkers, biologists Bill Stiver and Charles (Chuck) Hester, to share their job responsibilities and thoughts on wildlife management. All three were conscientious employees, and I thought of them as successful role models for my aspiring followers.

These students were able to view some rather high-tech firearms that were secured in a safe there but seasonally brought out and used for hog eradication efforts. Another little-know area was the storage area where stale donuts were on the ready as irresistible temptations for luring cantankerous bears into culvert traps when the need arose.

More than once when we were with a gathering of these eager scholars, I heard Kim say that he did not feel it was a good idea to "humanize" bears by assigning them names normally ascribed to two-legged creatures. I agreed.

It is likely through this kind of casual association that some individuals become too nonchalant in the presence of bears to maintain their objectivity, eventually bringing harm to both themselves and undeserving animals. Former Great Bear Foundation acquaintance Timothy Treadwell met his tragic death in this manner in October 2003 along Alaska's Katmai coast.

Though Timothy no doubt enjoyed a special relationship with some of North America's largest land carnivores, these "gentle giants" savagely killed and consumed both Timothy and his female companion, Amy Huguenard. Sadly, this was her initial voyage to Katmai to experience what Timothy found euphoric.

Restraint is often derived from experience, but this was 1982, and for Kathy and me in these Smoky Mountains, it was early in our tenure among bears. The name "Bertha" was thus assigned to a particular mother bear that we would see on numerous summer visits this season. Much would change in the coming years in how the two of us would view bears and how nuisance bear management would evolve.

The thinking of the period was to remove a troublesome bear from a site after a repeat episode of property destruction, or worse, a threat to a visitor. This relocation of a bear to some other more remote area of the park was labor intensive. Often, the offender made a gallant return, only to be quietly euthanized when the behavior repeated itself.

As bear management has evolved, fewer problem bears are relocated; rather, they are simply dealt with harshly at the site of offense to convince them that human interaction should be avoided. This more successful form of discipline still involves considerable time in the field by park employees.

Routinely, a bear is lured (donuts!) into a culvert trap, where after being sedated it is subjected to a rather crude tooth extraction for aging purposes back in the lab. The tooth is yanked from the jawbone. Blood and hair samples are taken to determine the presence of parasites or disease. Often, the lip is tattooed and stained, and at least one earflap is punctured and tagged with a colored and numbered metallic clamp to identify the culprit. The lip tattoo is a permanent mode of identification, obviously viewed up close while a captured bear is under sedation. Ear tags may become lost but are indicators of familiar bears from a safe distance when intact.

This field work-up is tantamount to humans having an annual physical where every orifice is indignantly and uncomfortably poked and explored in search of infirmity or disease. We tolerate these invasive insults by our internist for the sake of longevity. At the close of our visit, we gasp at the sight of the billing for multiple procedures and tests of our fluids.

Theory holds that bears view this form of quality time with a biologist as undesirable, also. After the work-up, bears are hastily shooed away, further reducing the likelihood that they will return to the area where they were initially captured.

We would encounter Bertha on several occasions over the summer around Spence Field. We could identify her by her colorful ear tags, and she seemed to tolerate us well even though she had two cubs-of-the-year at her side.

"Cubs-of-the-year" is an expression used to denote the current year's cubs as opposed to older "yearlings" or "sub-adults." Sometimes mother bears with young cubs will also have one or more older offspring still traveling with her.

These older hangers-on family members are akin to college graduates who still live at home and have not made it a priority to find a place of their own or secure a job. Such four- and two-legged "cubs" simply needed to move on in search of a life of their own. Often, bears are harsher in convincing cubs of this reality than softhearted human parents who might have also struggled to find their purpose in life.

There were only the two of us on this trip, and the park reservation system allowed twelve hikers to stay at the Spence Field shelter where there was a narrow, hard wire "bunk" space for each one. Therefore, there was a good probability that other hikers would show up as the afternoon gave way to evening.

This was a hot summer day, and we were soaked with perspiration and smelly from the five-mile climb up the Bote Mountain trail. We learned early in our hiking experiences that it was a good idea to drop our packs and clean up before we cooled down after reaching our destination. Once we relaxed a while and got comfortable, the idea of facing the inevitable cold water from a mountain stream led to dreading a bath.

Over the years, we had experienced many backpackers who chose not to bathe regularly, and we found it disgusting. First, how could anyone tolerate slipping into a sleeping bag while all damp and grimy? Then, how could one possibly sleep under such conditions? Though much of the world's less fortunate population does every night.

I always found that even if I only had enough water to wash my face and neck or sponge off a bit all over that I slept better. It also seemed that if I went to bed dirty, I never could get warm and was uncomfortable all night.

Regardless, for many years we have slept in silk long johns regardless of the season. We found that since silk was very slick and the sleeping bag interior surface was also, that moving about during sleep seldom woke us. In addition, the silk barrier between our skin and the bag keeps the bag cleaner, thus reducing the frequency of having to clean it, and therefore extending its longevity. Finally, silk is very light, thin, and easily washed and dried while on the trail. Sometimes, I have put it back on wet after washing, and it was dry in less than an hour from body heat.

It always took me less time to clean up in cold water than Kathy. I was a coward when it came to dousing my entire frame with the frigid liquid. She would scream and holler every time we went through this routine together, but she was much more thorough than I was.

A bath taken with cold water was always invigorating, to say the least. It always felt so good after the shock of cold water diminished.

After my bath and filling my water bottles for the evening's meal, I was to stand guard up the trail back toward the shelter just in case any later-comers ventured down toward the water source while Kathy was having her bath. At least that is what I heard her say before she disappeared to the stream.

The watering hole was seventy-five yards or so downhill and behind the shelter, and the trail to it continued down the mountain for about eight miles to Fontana Lake. This was the Eagle Creek trail, and having hiked it only once with two other friends from the Lake up to Spence Field, we had renamed it "Evil Creek." There were numerous creek crossings, and the elevation gain is over three thousand feet.

In our outdoor jaunts over the years, we had encountered more bears along the ridgeline of this region between Spence and Russell Field to the west than anywhere else in the Smokies.

Numerous bears traveled the two-plus mile corridor between the shelters along the famed Appalachian Trail. No doubt, they were in pursuit of the abundant serviceberry trees that adorned the ridgeline, from which bears made a living on the tasty fruits.

Kathy was cleaning up after the strenuous five-mile hike from Cades Cove to the shelter, soaked with sweat from hiking in the August heat and humidity. She had filled a pot from a short piece of pipe embedded in the bank that channeled the water flow. Occasionally, this welcome assist was made of PVC or fashioned cleverly from a slab of bark.

We always used a pot or two to collect water, and then stepped well away from the water source to bathe. This served to reduce the possibility of wastewater making its way back into the source and contaminating it for future users, both man and beast. In addition, this was in accordance with park regulations, which we respected.

Water sources in the high country were often just a trickle and unreliable during the months of July and August. This particular source had always been dependable, if sometimes slow.

Because earlier we had heard that bears were frequenting the area, I had been directed to be on watch up the hill toward the shelter in case one might venture down to where Kathy was bathing. Kathy would say that "because I was a man," I had not listened.

I interpreted her instructions to mean that I was to watch for, and stall, any hikers who came down for water, else they would discover her nude during her bath. This possibility did seem more likely. I also must confess that I envisioned her youthful form as it was exposed in the filtered light—a distraction from the assigned duty, but a pleasing one!

Kathy selected a bathing spot away from the stream, prepared her toiletries and clean clothes, filled a pot with water, and began the ceremony. After stripping down to her flip-flops and commencing to remove the day's dirt, she needed more water to complete the task, so back to the stream.

Bertha was a sizeable bear, but she had silently sauntered up the hillside through summer's lush understory and paused directly behind Kathy. Bending over to refill her pot, Kathy peered back and was surprised to discover an upside down image of an inquisitive Bertha awaiting her turn at the watering hole. There she stood, close enough that Kathy could sense the steamy breath against her wet cheeks.

Oh my! This presented quite the predicament, as Kathy was not properly attired to leave her post. It was Bertha's domain, and she simply wanted to quench her thirst. Only Kathy or the bruin could comfortably occupy this oasis at a time and fulfill their intended mission. That was the issue at hand.

The two of them had to agree on who held the most authority. Kathy slowly and quietly righted herself, not knowing how Bertha would react to her spoiling the bruin's desire to drink. Her heart raced as the closeness of this encounter did not provide a suitable retreat, and certainly not a modest one.

In situations such as this, those new to the outdoor scene might have screamed and darted into the underbrush only to be pursued, but not so this fledgling hiker. She was a veteran of at least a few other close encounters, most of them hapless blunderings. Here, calmness, and perhaps a sense of oneness with nature prevailed.

Kathy simply stood there confidently as the cold water dripped down her face and gave Bertha time to assess an alternative suitable to both parties. The outcome in such drama is always the decision of the bear.

Clearly, she was in the midst of what Bertha had journeyed up the hill to find. Kathy's presence must have given Bertha pause to reconsider her degree of thirst.

Foregoing the customary "huff" and chomping of teeth that were highly effective in such predicaments, Bertha methodically turned and ambled back down the hillside from which she had come. She did this as if to say, "Oh, go ahead and finish bathing. I'll come back later."

Bertha yielded to this higher form of life through avoidance behavior and slipped out of sight. Perhaps several years of experience assured this bear that Kathy was not a threat. Retreat preserved more energy than confrontation.

I would not hear of this moment with Bertha until Kathy had completed her bath, and the two of us made our way back to the shelter. After sharing this brief, exhilarating experience, she thoroughly chastised me for my inability to follow directions and failing as sentry. Her thoughts continued on Bertha for the evening while mine were still of this bathing beauty!

CHAPTER 9

BEARS OF THE NOONDAY SUN

*Sometimes a bear not actually seen
can be the most thrilling.*

*We had walked up this portion of the grassy roadway no
more than thirty minutes beforehand, and I know we did
not miss this. There it was in the middle of our path. It
was fresh, black, full of seeds, and still steaming in the cold
air—a big heap of bear scat.*

North Carolina's Nantahala National Forest is 531,148 acres of rugged, mountainous terrain, hosting a plethora of understory flora and fauna.

The precipitous ridges often hide their valleys and deep gorges from sunlight until morning gives way to mid-day, thus creating ravines carpeted with lush, moist greenery. The Cherokee Indians native to this region adeptly haled it "Nantahala," Land of the Noonday Sun.

This mostly temperate deciduous forestland is also home to an abundance of amphibians, reptiles, fish, small game, and four big game mammal species: white-tailed deer, wild hog, turkey, and black bear.

As early as April 1975, I was rambling around in the Joyce Kilmer Memorial Forest portion of this vast landscape. Joyce Kilmer Forest lies within the Joyce Kilmer-Slickrock Wilderness of Nantahala and is comprised of 17,394 acres of protected woodland.

What is most noteworthy about Joyce Kilmer, aside from the balance of the Nantahala forest, is the abundance of its impressive old growth trees, mostly yellow poplar. These stately centurions, like their predecessors the American chestnuts, once dominated the Southern Appalachians before extensive logging in the late 1800s and early 1900s.

The enormous chestnut hardwoods gave way to a parasitic blight brought into this country in 1904 and consequently decimated the chestnuts throughout the East. The chestnut was not only a valued source of lumber, fence rails, and firewood for early settlers, but was a significant food source for both man and beast.

Pioneers prized the chestnut wood for its resistance to decay and praised the meat of its nuts for food and substance for livestock—hogs. It was revered as "shoe money" when sacks gathered by numerous offspring were sold for income. Cash bought items not made in remote hollows but needed for survival and comfort, like coffee, salt, soda, sugar, and of course, shoes.

Most widely known as a poet, Mr. Joyce Kilmer penned one of America's most insightful poems, *Trees,* and it had a profound impact on the development of my view of the natural world. Kilmer also served his country in World War I as a journalist and was killed in action by a sniper's round. Afterwards, the Veterans of Foreign Wars petitioned the government to set aside a fitting forest stand as a living memorial to him, and thus the Joyce Kilmer Memorial Forest we enjoy today was created.

In 1971, four years out of graduate school, I began discovering the many gems of this remarkable forest. Over the ensuing years, I would make the region a regular backpacking destination with others.

One fall overnight camping trip to Bob Stratton Bald is still firm in my memory. Several friends and I camped on the bald and endured a cold, rainy night before departing for home the next day. Rain was common in the fall, and this was a particularly vicious storm. It savagely thrashed our tents throughout the night as we slept in a tight wad for fear of being blown from the exposed meadow.

Soon after returning home, we learned that a small plane had crashed, killing all four occupants. It was said that the plane went down near Bob Bald the night we were there. Throughout the years, we would continue to learn of other flights and dreams cut short by the ruggedness of those mountains and their unforgiving weather.

I knew there were bears there, and sometime later, on a hike up to Hangover Lead Overlook, I found a decaying bear head stuffed over a tree stump. Although a gruesome discovery, I suspected that it was simply placed there after someone found the carcass or the head portion.

Even though these mountains were well known for exceptional fall bear and hog hunting, I recall encountering little more than an occasional dog or seedy-looking hunter. Reflecting back, it seems that the hunters generally confined themselves to the valleys, and hikers tended to seek the mountain crests. Therefore, there was never any perceived conflict between a mix of firearms and adventurists.

These hunting dogs were always ugly, mottled hounds and, though lanky and thin, seemed a bit threatening and likely to take a bite of you if given the opportunity. Most of those hunting dogs even back then sported radio collars with a short antenna whip that allowed hunters and dogs to stay connected. The electronic collars have been improved substantially over the years, but the dogs continue to be *ugly*. For the most part, the gauntness still prevails.

When my group would encounter one of these disoriented hounds in the woods, some empathetic soul would predictably want to lead it out. They would weaken at the sight of an exhausted and hungry warrior and then feel compelled to get it back to its owner.

Befriending the canine with carry-out scraps pulled from the backpack, they would discover a brass nameplate riveted to the dog's collar. Using the information, they would call the owner at the first opportunity down the road, since cell phones did not exist at the time.

After a few of these learning experiences, it became apparent to me that there was no need. Some calls seemed to annoy the owners, and others responded, simply asking that we tie the hound to a guard rail where they would retrieve it.

Abhorring the thought, my friends balked at the concept. Realizing there was no other alternative, they complied and begrudgingly departed for home, leaving the dog behind. They were valuable dogs, and the hunters always reconnected with them, even if they had been several days on the loose. There was honor among these mountain people. If not found by the intended owner, another hunter who recognized "that dog" would see that it got back home.

During these initial 1970s explorations, it was easy to recognize where bears had clawed and chewed almost every wooden trail sign within Joyce Kilmer. Sometimes, signs would be reduced to kindling. I found this amusing, but I was confident that the individual who labored up the mountain to place the sign did not appreciate the infraction.

Later, I came to recognize diggings, gutted trees, and droppings of bears as my awareness and knowledge of them increased. Bears are consummate opportunists, seldom passing up the temptation to flip over and explore under a large rock or decayed log for ants, larvae, or a savory amphibian.

It pains me still to think that they dig up fall's yellow jacket nests for the minimal nutrition found within. Apparently, the reward of these treats exceeds the suffering to gather them. Beekeepers in bear habitat know all too well that bears will destroy a hive for the sugary goo, despite the vehement defense they encounter.

As my relationship with Kathy developed in the early 1980s, we made a number of excursions to the Joyce Kilmer area, mostly hiking with like-minded friends and coworkers of mine from college teaching.

Our enjoyment of this area would continue over the years that followed. She eagerly accompanied me as I took many college and university groups to Joyce Kilmer. These mountainous excursions quickly sorted out the fit from the lethargic, but no one, upon surviving these marches, complained of their beauty and diversity of life.

On a 1990s summer hike with a friend along the Slickrock Creek Trail, the two of us came upon a young bear just sitting in the woods adjacent to the trail. I vividly recall that we were returning from Lower Falls after an overnight backpacking trip. As we walked out of camp that morning, we encountered the bear.

My friend Bruce had never seen a bear. Initially, I did not see this one. With my head to the ground and more concern for copperheads or rattlesnakes, I walked right past this bear.

As I continued in the lead, Bruce, with a rather quiet voice, said, "There's a bear."

For someone who had never seen one, and now to be right next to it, he was not the least bit energetic or alarmed about his discovery. The bear was equally disinterested in the two of us and simply gave us a pass as it sat upon its haunches just off the trail.

Big Huckleberry Knob

Our best route to this area from our East Tennessee town was US Highway 129, which ran along the northeast perimeter of the wilderness. With easier access to that area, we paid little attention to what was occurring on the other side of the Wilderness, the completion of the Cherohala Skyway.

What I knew of this government pork project I did not like at the time, for it was to gut its way right through the middle of this mountainous haven for wild things. Ultimately, it would take more than thirty years and one hundred million dollars to bring it to fruition in October 1996.

Though the official Cherohala Skyway is only thirty-six miles in length, the mountainous highway winds continuously for fifty miles, connecting the rural communities of Robbinsville, North Carolina, to the east and Tellico Plains, Tennessee, to the west. It winds and turns sometimes almost into itself, and at intervals, portions of it take the traveler above 5,400 feet. As one of the highest highways east of the

Mississippi, it splices North Carolina's Nantahala National Forest from Tennessee's only national forest, Cherokee National Forest.

The sparsely settled town of Robbinsville is surrounded by the Nantahala Forest, and Tellico Plains lies adjacent to the Cherokee Forest. Thus, with the intent of increasing commerce and tourism between the two forested communities, the highway, named "Chero-hala" for the two forests, came to life.

By far, it is more of a gold brick road across gems of majestic green tapestry than an expressway for noisy delivery trucks and hordes of tourists descending upon quiet valleys to purchase "Indian" moccasins made in China. Traveling between the two communities offers the interloper splendid views of mountain ridges and deep gorges, brilliantly colored in the fall and snow-white in the wintertime.

Aside from the eye-catching scenery along the Skyway, there are numerous pull-offs allowing venturesome individuals access to a number of trails into both bear-inhabited forests. Trails near the sleepy town of Robbinsville lead to two historic balds, Hooper and Huckleberry. Both commonly offer scatterings of coyote, hog, and bear sign to those observant and in the know.

Hooper Bald rises to 5,429 feet, and it was on the bald that an early entrepreneur named George Moore established a rustic hunting lodge in 1912, complete with bison, elk, grizzly, mule deer, pheasants, turkeys, and wild hogs loosely confined within a five-hundred-acre chestnut split-rail enclosure.

In a short time, Moore became disenchanted with the ill-fated venture and sold the two-thousand-acre parcel to his manager, Garland "Cotton" McGuire. Most of the animals would soon perish from their new inhospitable environment, but sufficient wild hogs would escape, survive, and populate the surrounding woodlands.

By the 1940s, these well-established gregarious herds would give rise to what are currently hunted today in both states. They also would become a nuisance issue for adjacent Great Smoky Mountains National Park north of the region.

Because the hogs are considered destructive aliens within the preservation mandate of the parkland, an eradication program has been in existence for decades, holding their numbers to a tolerable limit. To date ten thousand hogs have been removed from within the park through trapping and hunting, but only by park rangers.

Sadly, perhaps Big Huckleberry Knob, a little higher than Hooper at 5,560 feet (and the highest point in North Carolina's Graham County), is known historically for the two drunks, Andy Sherman and Paul O'Neil, who perished near there. Setting out from the Tellico River for Robbinsville on a snowy, bitter-cold day on December 11, 1899, they became intoxicated, then lost. Their bodies would not be discovered until the following September 6 by a deer hunter. Afterward, an inquest directed that O'Neil's remains be used as a medical exhibit and those of Sherman, mangled by wild critters, were to be buried atop Huckleberry in a simple grave. In 1988, a short story of their fate was filmed there, entitled "Dead Man's Run," and aired on national television.

We have made numerous trips along the one-mile stretch to the Knob hiking with guests from Snowbird Mountain Lodge, which is located about eight miles east on the Cherohala. Aside from cozy lodging, fabulous dining, and the ambiance one would expect from a historic, rustic lodge, we have made great friends there while entertaining them as guests.

There are often interesting finds prevalent along this trail up to Huckleberry. To the observant hiker on most trails, it is common to note more than one pile of coyote scat. Often, all that remains of it after a rain or two is a twist of fibers, sometimes mangled with black hair; is it bear or hog? Well, only serious investigators would dare scrutinize it closely, but sometimes the reward for the curious is greater than the awkwardness of handling droppings of another being (Kathy will have no part of this and *always* carries hand sanitizer) – yuk!

What often is assumed to be bear hair in coyote scat may prove to be hog hair if fibers are carefully viewed and found to include some with split ends. Though both bear and hog hair is often dark, such additional evidence delineates hog hair from that of bear. A cape of split-end hair bolsters a larger-than-life stature for the hog, allowing it to appear more foreboding to potential foe.

In the Nantahalas, we occasionally found hair from both black bear and wild hog in the same scat, suggesting that the coyote was privy to carrion from each within a short time. It is unlikely that a coyote would kill an adult bear or sizeable hog. But a cub or piglet, or an old or injured adult, might fall victim to the opportunist.

A few years ago, on an April day, we repeated the journey to Big Huckleberry as green grass was just beginning to overtake the ruts of the approach from our parked vehicles. We enjoyed the views, shared various distant points of interests with our guests, and took pictures before departing.

Heading back down the ridge toward the parking lot, we came upon a distinctive pile of dark scat in the middle of the trail. What distinguished these droppings from similar finds beforehand was that they were fresh!

We had walked this same path just a short time ago. I was sure that we had not walked over this obvious mound. It was black, full of seeds, but the kicker was that it was still steaming!

For certain, bears use our trails. Had the bear followed us as we hiked out or darted ahead as we plodded along on our return and just defiantly pooped in the trail to acknowledge our trespass? We would never know, but a bear had just been there.

In all likelihood, the sly bruin had evaluated and intuitively dismissed this parade of two-legged intruders with impunity as they do so often, undetected.

CHAPTER 10

HUMAN CANNONBALL

Darkness was beginning to overtake the shelter, and most everyone now lay in their sleeping bags staring through the chain link fence in hopes of seeing some action. No one could have anticipated what was about to happen, as the bear advanced…

Tricorner Knob shelter is located just off the Appalachian Trail in the eastern end of Great Smoky Mountains National Park. It is favorably perched for protection from the weather against an embankment at 6,120 feet and situated just below Mt. Hardison. Given the high elevation, it is always a cool place on summer evenings and can be bitterly frigid in the wintertime.

There is often something surreal about its misty surroundings, which results from the enormous canopy of tree-life exuding a blanket of fog from nature's transpiration process within the leaves. Even during the winter season when these leafless forms stand as naked, gray sentries, heavy, ivory clouds often prevail, adding to the mystique of a cold night's stay there.

The backcountry site's water source conveniently originates from a spring less than thirty feet from the shelter's entrance. Frequently, such water sources are also known to be stops for thirsty bears.

Generally, water is directed by a pipe placed in the flow as the spring erupts from a dirt bank. I say "generally," because various attempts are made from time to time to improve such water outputs along the trail. These amateur creative feats are performed by hyperactive campers who either arrive early at shelters with too much free time before night falls or become frustrated when the existing apparatus is not functioning appropriately. I learned a long time ago not to trifle with these fragile engineering marvels, because quite often, my adjustments only muddied the water and extended the time it took to obtain it.

Kathy and I were conducting a Smoky Mountain Field School session this particular summer with mostly novice hiking participants. This was an educational cooperative offering between the University of Tennessee and the National Park Service.

Our advertised agenda consisted of a week's hike beginning at the park's eastern end at Davenport Gap, an hour's drive east from Knoxville, Tennessee. We would backpack for thirty miles along the crest of the AT to the park's near-midpoint of Newfound Gap and our awaiting vehicles.

This was a rigorous undertaking even for the more experienced hikers within our group, though we were taking five days to complete the task. Our itinerary would have us stop overnight at each of the four shelters along the route.

Overnight stays along the AT within the Smokies required the use of shelters. Obtaining a backcountry permit required one individual from the party to designate a specific shelter for each night's stay. No more than one night could be spent at each shelter, and the entire party was limited to eight participants.

The free permit system, implemented in the 1970s, was to limit the impact at heavily used areas like Tricorner Knob shelter. The NPS being an extension of the federal government (under the Department of Interior—it was always a mystery to Kathy that the DOI dealt with everything outside), no doubt also used the permit system to collect endless data about park use.

Because hiker vehicles left unattended at Davenport Gap were known to be routinely vandalized, we chose to park down the mountain a short distance at the Big Creek Ranger Station. This required a two-mile hike out of the gap along Chestnut Branch Trail until it joined the AT about the same distance west of Davenport.

The first day with any group is always the most difficult, because most participants do not know each other and we seldom are acquainted with all of them or their capabilities as backpackers. Everyone was tired by day's end, but otherwise we had an uneventful stay at the first shelter, Cosby Knob.

After an eight-mile hike, the water source located close to the shelter was a welcome sight. One only had to walk fifteen or so paces to the natural earthen basin that constantly filled and overran from a pipe similar to that which would be found at Tricorner. On a rainy arrival, with dinner not too distant a thought, this was a celebrated convenience indeed.

The only downside to the water sources at both shelters was that they were located a little too close, raising the possibility of human contamination from a quick pee (or worse!) in the night from a not-so-conscientious explorer. It only took a stay or two at most to convince me of the need to treat all water found at such locations.

This mindset was based vividly on a quarter of college parasitology as I neared graduation in the late 60s. I did not want to be heaving from one end or spewing from the other because of someone's carelessness in the backcountry. I could recall more than one occasion on wintertime treks where bending forward or squatting in deep snow for relief just from indigestion added to the misery of an already unpleasant calling.

We found this trip to be interesting immediately on meeting our group for the first time in the parking lot. All seemed like great folks, and some had no experience, while at least one other had considerable miles behind him.

What was more intriguing than the personalities was the plethora of rain suits that quickly came out at the first sight of drizzle. This was on our second day together headed toward Tricorner Knob just below the summit of Mt. Guyot at 6,621 feet, the second-highest peak in the park.

Today, there is no distinct trail to the top of Guyot. I can remember noticing a disturbed path for a number of years leading off the AT before it became overgrown for a lack of park maintenance. I have a photographic slide of the sign that used to mark the trail's departure from the AT and remember well once making my way to the top for a disappointing view. The sign noted the distance of three-quarters of a mile, and though overgrown and brushy, I seriously doubted that it was that far.

The weather always seemed harsher at Tricorner Knob, and with regularity, it seemed to rain on us when we passed along the shoulder of Guyot. The season did not matter, except for when we plodded along on ice or tramped through heavy snow. Arriving with this group supported the rain theory once again.

Linda Lee, a first-timer from Ohio along with her husband Dick, became our initial concern. Most of us were chilled to the bone and wet from perspiration and the prevailing moisture, but Linda was noticeably warm-natured. Her grossly inadequate rain jacket, one I would ask for and keep as an example of what not to use in future backpacking classes, just disintegrated early into our rainy hike.

It was one of those items a person might purchase in a weak moment at Wal-Mart to keep in the car in case they were caught in a downpour while grocery shopping. Anyone having experienced a run to the car with an armload would realize quickly that it was insufficient for even that. It did not provide adequate coverage and would tear—which it did on this trip—the minute any stress was placed on the seams. It was vinyl and would crack or just split right off of you, like it did Linda at the arms.

First, I would not have owned such a useless item, and second, if I had, I would have been frantic at the loss of its minimal protection from the rain, but not Linda. She simply removed the whole thing and walked in the drizzle as steam poured from her overheated torso and bare arms.

My thought was that she would soon lapse into hypothermia, ruin the trip for everyone, and we would be sued for our irresponsibility in allowing her to come in the first place. However, she would prove to be a trooper—a hot-bodied trooper—who would stay comfortable even if the balance of us were not.

Her husband Dick would accompany Kathy and me for hundreds of miles in the years to come, as he, along others met on such ventures, attempted to complete the entire AT. In our hiking clique of eight, we affectionately would come to call him "Big 'Un."

Dick was a large man who towered over me, and I am six feet tall. He appeared rather rough and even scary, I thought. Underneath this image though, was a lamb, a teacher with a kind persona that we would come to cherish. He also had a sense of humor, and so the majority of us would abuse him relentlessly on our future trips together.

Also on this trip was Joyce Rogers from Clinton, South Carolina. She seemed to make the city of Clinton a complete sentence with her delightful Southern drawl. On this first trip with her, we would ask her repeatedly to tell us where she lived so we could hear her talk.

Joyce was a pretty, loveable blonde and would prove to be a strong hiker with noteworthy experience. We would become close friends, and she also would accompany us on several trips in the years yet to come.

The other extreme in our group was a novice, a fellow who obviously had purchased a high-end Eddie Bauer Gore-Tex® rain suit just for this, his virgin trip. Gore-Tex® was just beginning to make a serious appearance in the market as a suitable material for rain gear. The suit was teal green in color, immaculate. The pants almost seemed to have been pressed.

This color, I thought, was rather gaudy for wilderness gear but was more befitting for the pages of an Eddie Bauer catalog just to make some sort of outdoor fashion statement. It was what one would expect to see in a slick catalog on a handsome New York model who was eyeing some imaginary point in the distance as if he had a lust for the wilderness. The experienced reader would know that such feet had never been off paved streets.

The teal suit would prove to be comical, as quickly this fashion statement would become trashed by the debris kicked up from a muddy trail in nature's defiance. He was what Kathy and I called a "kicker," a person who hiked in such a manner as to wash down the inside of their pant legs with mud on each step.

The whole inseam of these teal rain pants, from the cuffs to the crotch, would become streaked with brown trail mud. It would not likely come out after repeated washings back home, either. So the wearer would be identified for as long as they wore those pants as a "kicker" by those who also saw the humor in this.

By the time we arrived at Tricorner, everyone was soaked. It was a combination of perspiration trapped inside rain gear from the arduous hike and the rain that eventually penetrated the outside fabric from hours of drizzle. We found that those who had carefully chosen the better gear stayed dry the longest, but eventually everyone became wet and cold.

The shelters along the AT in the Smokies are mere three-sided lean-tos that mostly provide protection from extremes in wind, rain, or snow. They are not luxurious destinations with a warm cabin atmosphere, but at the time consisted of hard wire bunks and muddy dirt floors that would be frozen solid in winter. Today, hikers find that the wire has been replaced with wooden planks, less likely to snag expensive gear and provide more comfort. For many of their thirty-plus years of existence, the shelters have been in various stages of neglect and deterioration.

Since we had tolerated this for many excursions through the park, we knew the urgency of arriving at our nightly destinations early enough to claim the primo spots. Arriving in the early afternoon could mean the difference between tolerating a constant drip from a leaky metal roof in a prevailing rainstorm, having to crowd up against a cold, dusty wall laden with mouse droppings, or sleeping in a relatively dry, moderately comfortable space.

My strategy had always been to lay claim to an available space near the cleanest of the right or left walls to ensure that I would not be sandwiched between one or more "snorers, tossers, or gassers" who might venture in later. I could better cope with the mouse issues than most.

I would unfurl my sleeping pad and fluff my bag to ensure the greatest possible flexibility for enduring the night, because to this day I have never slept well in shelters. I could place my light source, container of water, hat, and additional clothes near my head for easy reach while semi-comatose in the early morning.

Today, those shelters along the trail in the Smokies have all been completely renovated and improved considerably. This has been an extraordinary accomplishment by a host of dedicated and skillful volunteers with limited assistance from a much reduced staff and financially strapped Park Service. Many of the shelters enjoy a new roof; expanded cooking surfaces well outside the sleeping quarters; and even acrylic skylights that almost beckon one to stay a second night, which is taboo in this park. The work of these individuals is to be admired and appreciated by every visitor to these shelters.

Once we established our presence for the evening, wet clothes quickly were dispatched in trade for warmer wool and the newer polyester fabrics just beginning to make their way into the market. The synthetics were slow to give up vital warmth and dried more quickly than earlier wool clothing, which left the hiker smelling like a wet dog.

Surprisingly, few in this group had any cotton garments. Cotton, even back then, was well known to be a killer of outdoors persons by leading to hypothermia when it acquired moisture and collapsed as an insulating barrier.

As I recall, no other hikers showed up that evening. As darkness approached, we seemed to have the shelter to ourselves. There was never any assurance that some poor souls would not be "off-permit" (or never had one) and slide in as we prepared our dinner, or worse, clicked off the last light source.

At the shelters, it was always nice to have our groups to ourselves without the need of explaining to strangers who we were and where we all lived. Kathy would repeatedly remind me that our guests enjoyed that, but I found the distraction annoying.

We always counseled our participants to avoid sharing too much information with other hikers along the trail and at campsites. I would insert that they did not have to be unfriendly or rude, but we should be cautious. I would warn that disseminating too much information about our timeframe, destination, and beginning and ending points might lead to vandalism of vehicles at either end of our hike or some other form of harm to our group.

Sometimes they took this to the extreme. It was almost funny at times when they were asked something by a trail stranger; they would become mute and nod toward one of us. They would do so as if they just knew they would be outwardly scolded should they eke out an improper response.

Dinner was a mix of us eating within the dimly lit confines of the shelter and those just outside the gated bear fence that separated bruin from hikers. There was no campfire that night, only the loud hissing and blue glow from backpacking stoves of the period.

Meals were laboriously prepackaged and neatly labeled for each day by Kathy before we departed home. This was done and included as part of the session fee to save weight and ensure that some fool did not pack weighty cans for an entire week. We also furnished the cook gear and stoves because invariably someone would bring their own stove, it would not work, and they would look to us to fix it. Upon initially meeting our group, we would distribute each group of four's food and cook gear for the week and ask that they divide it equally among themselves to carry.

Early as a trip leader and instructor, I learned a couple of things in leading new participants. The first was to know your equipment and provide the basics for your group, as not to have four different stoves of unknown working order or six different tents where some were rentals that had the wrong poles or the fly of another tent design mistakenly packed with them (both actually happened).

Second, never stop on a bridge over a stream, because someone in the group most assuredly will drop something and expect you, the leader, to go after it. Once on a three-day Alaskan thirty-mile backpacking trip on the Kenai, actually with Big 'Un as our friendship had progressed, a younger guy in our group took off his boots while sitting on a bridge and dropped one of them into the swift water below. He looked up to me in astonishment, as if I were to blame and would become its savior. I screamed, "Go get it!"

At Tricorner Knob, it was getting dark, and we were finishing our meal when a medium-sized bear appeared not too distant from us in front of the water source. We hastened everyone toward the gate and into the shelter. We scrambled for all of our cook gear, too, so stoves and pots would not be destroyed by a curious snout and habituate the bear to human food.

In all the excitement, the bear disappeared, and everyone's focus turned to clean-up and preparing their sleeping space in anticipation of a cool damp night. Tired as we all were from a hard hike that day, we soon made our way into these sacks as twilight enveloped us. Most everyone, secure in their respective beds, flipped on their stomachs, and stared out through the mesh fence in anticipation of the bear's return. It was quiet now.

This was common practice on Smokies hikes, as the larger, more interesting animals—bears, deer, and sometimes hogs—became more active at dusk and occasionally visited a shelter site to see what they might find. Of course, this position also provided an opportunity to whisper secrets as couples, tell a joke to those still alert, or laugh at the ones quickest to begin snoring. An occasional skunk might also venture in just to test the beam of our lights and to inspect any unwashed pots left at ground level.

On a clothesline near the water pipe hung a few socks and a neoprene knee brace that had become an inseparable piece of my gear on every hike. My left knee had slowly degenerated from about age ten, when I had had a bicycle accident one night riding home in the dark from a friend's house. Back then, the road was a gravel one, and I had gone head over handlebars, injuring my elbow and knee.

Low-level chats and giggling common to such small group settings ceased when in a low voice someone murmured, "There's a bear." With most everyone awake now, the bear appeared a short distance from the water pipe and the overhanging clothesline.

As if somehow drawn to the equally dark form, the bear appeared fixated on the sweaty knee brace and advanced toward it. As soon as he had approached the line, he raised his head and extended his snout to grasp the brace.

Now, while the device was useful for its intended purpose, I did not see it important enough to warrant crawling out of my bag to defend my property. After all, this was a bear, and humans are supposed to respect, even fear them. Not so with Kathy!

As all of us lay there caught up in the excitement of the possible melodrama to follow, with the bear departing with a mouthful of sweaty black rubber, it was as if Kathy were shot from a cannon. Suddenly, she catapulted from the innards of her bag, sprang to her bare feet, and blazed through the chain link door, grabbing her nearby hiking stick in one swift vault.

The spontaneity of it all gave no time for rebuttal or warning on the dangers of confronting a bear. She was enraged and that bear was not going to take my knee brace!

As she sprinted toward the bear in a furor, swinging frantically her lean stick, the bear, seemingly in fear for its life, made a power move into the dark, leaving the brace secured on the line. Closing in on the bear and out of our sight, she chased it further into the deep, misty woods as it eventually outpaced her, never to be seen again that night.

Reappearing some moments later, clad only in her sleepwear and not the least bit distressed, she snatched the brace and socks from the line, chained the shelter gate behind her, and re-entered her bag as if the intense theatrics had never occurred. Every observer lay in complete disbelief as to what they had just witnessed.

The cannon had encased its feisty load once more, and sleep overtook us all.

CHAPTER 11

Head-On Collision—Well, Almost!

*Suddenly and without warning, I came face-to-face with a
mother bear and her diminutive cub.*

We had first backpacked the length of Virginia's Shenandoah
National Park, a 101-mile stretch of the Appalachian Trail, in
September 1984.

Shenandoah, fully established as a national park in December
1935, is a lean, elongated piece of land in upper Virginia. Hiking the
AT through it is much easier than packing through the Great Smoky
Mountains. The trail grade over rolling hills is less strenuous than the
steep ascents and descents found in the Smokies to the south.

This initial Shenandoah trip was from a southern beginning at
Rockfish Gap east of Waynesboro, Virginia, to the park's northern
terminus at Highway 522 just east of Front Royal, Virginia. I led a
small band of college students who had enrolled in a field biology

course that I taught early in my career at Roane State Community College.

I was an associate professor of biology, and on this trip, Kathy served as my assistant, having received her master's degree in biomedical engineering two years prior. By this point in our relationship, we had hiked enough together that we made a good team for such an undertaking.

My department dean, Dr. Anne Minter, was a perceptive administrator and insightful enough to acknowledge the need to have more than one adult leading a bunch of young outdoor wannabes on such an adventure. Since I had several young women along, Kathy also served as a mentor and successful role model for them.

Eight years later, the second completion of the AT through Shenandoah was broken into two trips and conducted as offerings through the Smoky Mountain Field School in June of 1992 and 1993. Both trips began at opposing ends of the park and terminated at Big Meadows, a large clearing in the midst of the park through which the AT passes north and south. It is complete with a restaurant, lodge, and extensive campground with showers. With its rustic amenities, it is a welcome destination for both hikers and travelers along Skyline Drive.

In 1992, the two of us led eight participants from the park's south end at Rockfish Gap northbound for about sixty-two miles to Big Meadows. The next year brought eight of us together to hike from the north end of the park at Highway 522 southbound about forty-six miles to Big Meadows. I led this trip alone, as Kathy could not participate due to her "real job" in the medical field.

Most of the near-200,000-acre park (over 300 square miles) is forested with hardwoods, ancestors of immense trees that once provided food, building materials, fence posts, and firewood for early settlers. Elevations range from 495 feet at its northern entrance to 4,050 feet atop Hawksbill Mountain, about four miles north of Big Meadows.

Between 1933 and 1942, ten camps of Civilian Conservation Corps worked and lived within or adjacent to the park, with no fewer than a thousand young men working on projects under supervision of the army. CCC crews eager for a day's wages in an era of hardship built trails, roadways, and facilities throughout the park. Much of their effort was concentrated on the one-hundred-foot right-of-way of Skyline Drive as it made its way through the mountains.

For those with an adventuresome heart, Shenandoah Park is blessed (or cursed) with two options for exploration. Its length is bisected by both the AT and a portion of the Blue Ridge Parkway known as Skyline Drive. Great Smoky Mountains is divided by the AT along its crest into Tennessee and North Carolina sides. Running perpendicular to the trail about mid-point of the park, Highway 441 connects Gatlinburg, Tennessee, and Cherokee, North Carolina.

The Blue Ridge Parkway extends 469 miles south, connecting the Smoky Mountains National Park with Shenandoah. As a Depression-era project of the New Deal, it became the nation's initial and most extensive rural parkway.

Skyline Drive is the only public roadway in Shenandoah and extends north and south for 105 miles, often crossed by the meanderings of the AT. There are only four entrances to the park, and thus Skyline Drive, and all visitors must pay an entrance fee, with the exception of those thru-hiking the Appalachian Trail.

Those with a greater inclination toward solitude and more friendly terrain than found in the Smokies find that the Appalachian Trail in Shenandoah provides ninety-five miles of quiet travel, mostly along the crest of the Blue Ridge. Though managed by the same National Park Service agency that protects GSM, regulations for hikers here are more relaxed, as annual visitation is just over two million, compared to over nine million in the Smokies.

For example, hikers may travel with their dogs leashed in Shenandoah and camp throughout the park without being confined to designated campsites and shelters, as within the Smokies. Likewise, as in the Smokies, a free permit is required for overnight camping, but unfortunately backcountry rangers employed to enforce regulations are about as scarce as the elusive Shenandoah salamander.

Aside from its intense beauty any season of the year, Shenandoah's three hundred square miles of forestland is home to a respectable population of big game mammals: turkey, white-tailed deer, and black bear. Seldom is a hike completed without startling a flock of turkey, which explodes into the air and quickly disappears from feeding along trailside slopes. Likewise, most visitors are greeted early in their travels roadside or afoot by numerous white-tails.

Several hundred of Virginia's five thousand to six thousand black bears call Shenandoah home. Black bears evolved in the forest, and so with keen senses and sharp, curved claws, they easily escape into tree canopies undetected. On our excursions in Shenandoah, we had averaged two bears per visit, and none up close.

A nicety of hiking the Appalachian Trail through the park is that one can periodically camp at an established campground with potable water and a shower, or better yet, stay in public wayside lodges if plans are made accordingly. It was not uncommon on our two thru-hikes of the park to stop by a wayside restaurant for breakfast or lunch and to "water-up" before disappearing back into the forest again in our pursuit of the next campsite for the evening.

One thing that I remember with certainty about our travels through the park is the uncanny number of Eastern timber rattlesnakes that we encountered. Sometimes, there is the need to place women and children up front when hiking, and rattlesnake country is one of those situations. On both the college trips and the field school trips, we did have our dog AT, and she was always good at discovering rattlers and alerting our group—but only after we were in their midst.

This is not to imply that Shenandoah boasts of a high population of these menaces to foot travel, but rather that we consistently saw more of them there than on any other hundred or so mile segment of the trail. Moreover, but not unique to Shenandoah, I insist that timber rattlers only come in large! The snort of a deer is startling while searching in the dark for a place to pee, but that sudden and distinctive buzz of a few rattles on the tail of a big rattler will be remembered forever.

I never recall seeing a small timber rattler in all of our explorations within the Southern Appalachians, extending all the way to New England, where serpents are said to become fewer in number. However, Kathy and I encountered non-poisonous varieties while hiking all the way through Maine on the AT.

The idea of hiking through Shenandoah National Park on the Appalachian Trail a third time came about early in 2008 for two reasons. First, I thought that I would like to do it one more time before I got to the inevitable point in the not-too-distant future where I would just be too old to make a rigorous backpacking trip. I was sixty now.

Second, it would be a fun and easy trip to do with our AT hiking friends. Also, they had hiked that portion of the trail without us. By the time we had met them in the mid-1990s, we had hiked it twice with others. So, they "slackpacked" (dayhiked) Shenandoah to catch up to where we had stopped in the mid-80s, just short of the Pennsylvania state line on our journey northward.

Therefore, seven of the eight of us were able to hike from Highway 522 southbound to Big Meadows in October 2008, spanning six days of backpacking. We averaged a little over seven and a half miles per day for the forty-six miles, short of our customary distance of twelve-plus miles a day, as on many other more challenging trips and twice the distance.

It was an invigorating time to be out. The air was dry, the nights were cool, and the trees were evolving toward their fall array of color. The weather was perfect—this was the reason you would ever go hiking in the first place.

The next year, June 2009, Kathy and I proposed that we backpack the southern section of the park. The distance of sixty-two miles was to be completed in seven days, averaging almost nine miles a day, still far less than the norm for this aggressive group.

Our AT group was comprised of Wayne Buchanan, Dick Lee, aka Big 'Un, Gene Robbins, Tom and Priscilla Siler, and Bill Williams, plus the two of us. Kathy was the youngest member of the group, since the balance of us were in our fifties and sixties. Tom and Pris made up the second couple of our group.

Now, this was no ordinary assemblage of friends completing a leisurely stroll. These individuals had proven themselves to be not only among the finest friends we could ever know in a lifetime, but strong, determined hikers who had seen life-threatening circumstances together, such as enduring 86-mph winds on the slopes of New Hampshire's Mount Washington as we made our way along the AT during 2004's Hurricane Frances.

Unlike the previous fall hike, it showered all week. By the time we had reached Loft Mountain Campground, some twenty-seven miles into our hike, Kathy's feet were blistered and bloody. Likely because of the trail's wetness, boots she had hiked in many miles beforehand began to gnaw at her toes and heels relentlessly the second day before arriving at Blackrock Hut.

This thirteen-miler would be our longest day of the excursion and an exhausting one for all of us. We stood in the rain to eat our dinner beside pitched tents in a designated site downhill from the shelter. Before retiring to our sleeping bags, we made our way down a steep bank along a precarious path to the creek for a cold bath amid scratchy brambles and drizzle.

By the time we had made the 7.4 miles further to Loft Mountain, Kathy had decided to stay in camp the next two days and help Dick's wife, Linda, shuttle us so that we could slackpack and return to Loft for a second and third night. While we were completing a section of the AT each day, Linda would dayhike other trails that she had researched. Kat rested her swollen feet without remorse.

I had reserved the Loft Mountain site online well ahead of our travels. The campground boasted of numerous flat tent sites, each with a large metal bear box nearby designed and anchored to allow secure storage of food and cooking gear should a curious bear wander through. A bathhouse was centrally located among the campsites, complete with dishwashing sink and even detergent and a scrubbing pad— unimaginable in a park so heavily used as the Smokies.

Each evening, Dick and Linda would return to a different area, since they had all their gear in their van and Dick dayhiked with us. That way Dick could join us early into a hike each day, walking in from the Skyway and going back out to the Skyway as we completed a day's journey; this was unique here where the trail and Skyway paralleled each other.

Before we would stay our last night at Lewis Mountain cabins then complete an easy walk of 8.7 miles to Big Meadows ending our trip, we would come face-to-face with one of Shenandoah's bruins and her cub. It was only a brief, hapless encounter, but it once more affirmed that these creatures were well adapted to their surroundings and instinctively knew how to cope with uninvited adventurers.

With Loft Mountain our third day's destination, we were stumbling down a portion of the AT narrowed on each side by a dense thicket of mountain laurel. The rocky trail required concentration in order to remain upright on both feet. Balance was compromised by our heavy backpacks and fatigue from a long day of hiking.

I was in the lead, and Bill's towering frame was close on my heels. He was in his customary "on a mission stupor" (when we were not solving global issues as we marched). Bill and I had always hiked out front, since both of us were long-legged and had a fast pace.

We turned a slight bend in the trail. Suddenly and without warning, I came face-to-face with a mother bear and her diminutive cub!

Small in stature, and yet daunting, the adult bear was not more than ten feet in front of me and coming in my direction with her cub behind her—on my Appalachian Trail!

Had I not changed focus from my feet on this arduous hike to venture a glance ahead, I never would have seen either of them. Because this encounter was so instantaneous, I never broke stride as I stammered to draw Bill's attention to what lay ahead.

By the time Bill had heard my feeble utterance of "Bears" and jerked his head upward to inquire, the mother bear and cub made a ninety-degree left turn. With the cub seemingly attached to her rump, in fewer than three "bear steps," they vanished into the heath.

All this happened within a matter of seconds without a pause, just avoiding us altogether. Bill got only a fleeting glimpse of their hindquarters as I deeply exhaled in amazement of what had transpired before us in so short a time.

We had been on a collision course. The moment our eyes met and each of us identified the intrusion, she skillfully had ushered her offspring out of what she must have perceived as harm's way and blended into the darkened cover of the laurel thicket.

Her tiny cub, close behind, never faltered in an almost robotic match of her every step, disappearing alongside. Within three steps of where I stood, she had led her cub and departed in a blink of the eye and without a uttering a sound or disturbing even the smallest twig.

This was her forest. She made a living here 24/7. Instinct drove her every move, and over thousands of years, a complex evolutionary process had provided her the skills she needed to avoid threats to both herself and her offspring. To us she symbolized wilderness, "the why we came," though bears are seldom experienced this closely.

The balance of our tired group, trudging behind Bill over the clatter of boots kicking up sharp stones, only heard that we had seen a bear. They never realized the mastery of escape that had played out right before us.

CHAPTER 12

Hayden Valley Encounters

We should not be here ...

This was Yellowstone—one of America's grandest national parks. I thought it was incredible to be standing there over the remains of a bison that had been ravaged by a grizzly. At least it was an interesting observation until Matt pointed to all the tracks in the area and his voice cracked.

Yellowstone National Park, established in 1872, is America's oldest national park and 2.2 million acres in size. It is difficult to grasp the immensity of the landscape and that it could be more than four times that of my Smokies.

Aside from its diversity of flora and fauna, Yellowstone features 10,000 hydrothermals, including 300 geysers. Said to have no wolves in 1994, more than 300 descendents from reintroduced ones in 1995 and 1996 roam its vast meadows and scrounge its mountains as predators in search of the living.

Spilling over into Idaho, Montana, and Wyoming, Yellowstone provides habitat to many of America's notable megafauna besides wolves, including black and grizzly bear, bison, elk, and moose. Likely, more than 300 of the Lower Forty-Eight's remnant of 1,000 grizzly bears find essentials for survival within its harsh, unforgiving environment.

While spring and summer months provide favorable temperatures for birthing and regaining strength from months of hibernation for many of its inhabitants, brilliant fall colors alert living things to an approaching winter of savage frigidity and layers of ice and snow that can be measured in feet. For humans well-appointed in the right gear, the winter wonderland that awaits provides glimpses of frozen waterfalls and wolf kills in paradise locations such as Lamar Valley.

My first trip to Yellowstone National Park was in August 1977, when we departed East Tennessee in my friend Terry Willard's pick-up truck bound for a two-week wilderness climbing and survival school.

Terry had seen an ad for Wilderness Institute, and this particular offering was to take place in the Cabinet Mountains of Idaho. Neither of us had ever been that far out West and certainly had never heard of the Cabinet Mountains, nor had we done any climbing.

Since we were heavily into backpacking, attending this school seemed like a good idea. So we paid our registration fees, filled out all of their forms, and we were off on a round-the-clock drive until arrival in Kalispell, Montana. A drive of this duration is tantamount to owning a pair of white shoes—once in a lifetime would suffice.

We reached Kalispell, near the Canadian border, thirty-five grueling hours later. Remarkably, though we were grumpy and our bodies atrophied, we were still speaking when we arrived there.

Three experienced leaders and climbers, Dick, Mitch, and Kathy, led the climbing and survival school. Dick was older than the rest of us, and the lead instructor. I remember that he wore the same clothes a lot but would sneak off every evening for a bath and do laundry while we set up camp. Mitch had a dark, full beard, and reminded me of the dwarfs in the Keebler cookie commercials. Kathy was the youngest among the three but a competent hiker and a good team builder.

We set out to backpack fifty miles off-trail within the Cabinet Mountains—prime bear habitat. Part of our time was to be spent learning new hiking and camping concepts. As we progressed across the Cabinets and came upon suitable rock cliffs, we engaged in climbing them to develop the skills of free-climbing and rappelling.

As part of our confidence-building experience, each of us was sent out in a different direction from our base camp to spend a night solo. We could only take water, a little food, a sleeping bag, and a few other essentials to have a truly primitive experience in bear country.

This was to be a first for all of us and a bit unnerving, since none of us knew the first thing about grizzly bears. Up to this time, I do not believe that I had ever camped alone before and only recall a few times since then.

As evening approached, I found a large boulder under which I could spread my sleeping bag and have my backside protected. Before darkness, I gathered an enormous stack of dried wood and built a roaring fire. Throughout the night, I was sandwiched between the boulder and the fire.

In theory, I thought that this was a clever idea to keep away any animals that might pose a threat, such as bears or mountain lions. It proved to be a long, boring, but thankfully, uneventful night. This dismissed any desires that I might have had for solo camping.

We learned a great deal about climbing, and for first-timers, I felt that we became admirably proficient at it for the time involved. Furthermore, how could anyone not enjoy the experience of learning here without the first distraction or influence from humankind? The craggy mountains were beautiful, and the sky was cobalt blue by day and sprinkled with countless stars at night.

We did not see any grizzlies on our adventure, but I vividly recall three other memorable events of our trip.

First, I insisted on riding in the back of our truck for the first leg of our journey. This would prove to be a mistake shortly before we were two miles from my home. Under the camper top with me was all of our hiking gear and clothing for the month-long outing, considerable food, and a number of two-liter soft drinks.   W e l l, for an unknown reason, one of the drink bottles just exploded, spewing its bubbly contents everywhere. Of course, it startled me. I did not know what had happened or, for an instant, where the noise originated. Immediately, a sticky, sugary mist covered me from head to toe, as well as all of our stuff, before we had even left Kingston.

Second, it was rather disheartening when our instructor, Kathy, experienced a free-climbing fall while demonstrating proper climbing technique to the rest of us. Our group of sixteen beginners stood speechless as the young alpinist tumbled from the rock wall. She was caught by her safety rope just before smacking the ground. Fortunately, she was roped in correctly, "on belay," and was not seriously injured, but she was so emotionally shaken that she hiked back out for home. I also believe she was exhausted from co-leading another session prior to ours.

Third, after an exhilarating adventure, we departed for home but took a side trip through Yellowstone National Park. In our group had been a fellow whose family had a condominium at Montana's Big Sky Lodge, so he suggested that we stay there and see some of the park.

We were completely taken with the landscape and wildlife found within Yellowstone, and of course, the geysers that abounded there. This country was more open and barren than our Smokies, where lush vegetation shrouds the landscape and a hazy mist looms during summertime. Here we saw bison, elk, and moose, and as every Yellowstone visitor must, we stood and gawked in astonishment as Old Faithful blew.

No less impressive were the Tetons and the splendor afforded by them. Of course, heading east we had to see Jenny Lake and stand beneath Grand Teton at 13,770 feet. Afterwards, we said good-bye to the West, made a stop at Missouri's Gateway Arch, and arrived back home on August 22. We had been changed for life by these experiences and harbored a determination to return to Yellowstone some day.

Sixteen years would pass before I would return to Yellowstone and see my first grizzly bear. This May 1993 adventure would be my initial face-to-face association with leaders and members of Great Bear Foundation. Three years later, Kathy and I would make a January trip to the northwestern corner and explore the Mammoth Hot Springs and Lamar Valley regions.

Beginning in 2003, we would for several successive years travel there in wintertime to cross-country ski with church friends, Richard and Ellen Bolen. So enamored with the offerings of this four-season playground for outdoors advocates, the Bolens sold their home in East Tennessee and relocated to the community of Emigrant, Montana, just outside Yellowstone's North Entrance.

For the May GBF foray, I met the group in Bozeman over breakfast, and we soon departed to see bears in both Yellowstone and Glacier National Parks. The session, entitled "Bears and Ecosystems Field Studies," was to be a six-day excursion.

Matt Reid, GBF Director of Programs and Fundraising at the time, would lead the Yellowstone portion of our week, and Dr. Chuck Jonkel, as GBF Founder, Scientific Advisor, and GBF membership newspaper *Bear News* editor, would lead the Glacier trip. Chuck wore a number of hats for GBF, and rightfully so, for the man had copious knowledge of the bear and its needs.

Wayne Buchanan (different from the "Wayne" who is mentioned elsewhere in the book regarding our hike of the Appalachian Trail), GBF President, would accompany us, along with biologist Steve Gehman, and four others like me. Each participant proved to have considerable knowledge about nature that each shared, and everyone was surprisingly, a good hiker.

On leaving Bozeman with all of us packed in a van for the several-hour journey to West Yellowstone, Matt chattered away about the bear. He seemed intent on sharing everything he knew with us and spewed volumes of useful and interesting information about the wildlife we would encounter, habitat, human encroachment, and of course, safety while traveling in bear country.

Entering Yellowstone after the Great Fires of 1988 at first proved depressing. Blackened skeletons of trees still remained in abundance, but as Matt related information to us about the significance of fire for rejuvenating understory food for animals, my focus turned to the impressive new growth that emerged beneath them.

The controversy continues to this day as to what the government should or should not have done over those several months that the park was ravaged by fire. Now, nature had rebounded, displaying a carpet of luxuriant growth that would provide well for Yellowstone's diverse and abundant wildlife.

Each of three days in Yellowstone consisted of a 6:00 am rise, then a quick breakfast, reload into the van for a drive to a new location, and a precursory hike of two to three miles to reach a different region of Hayden Valley. In daypacks, we carried our lunch, camera and bear viewing gear, and warm clothes. It was just the beginning of spring in some parts of the park, and one could become chilled sitting atop a knoll for hours, "glassing for bears."

Most national parks do not allow hunting or even firearms for personal protection. So there was also a canister or two of "bear spray" (pepper spray) carried along, for there would be the potential to encounter bears up close; after all, we had come in search of them. This pressurized form of a hot pepper mist was just beginning to make its way into the hiking and camping markets as a bear deterrent.

Hayden Valley was a primo spot for wildlife viewing because it was such rich habitat for animals, with its rolling hills and valleys interspersed with vast open meadows. One theory held that "bison rubs" on perimeter trees, often girdling them and resulting in their death, had kept them from encroaching upon these open spaces.

The limited summer warmth of May through August generally assures that road access will be unimpaired by ice and snow, and Hayden is only six miles from the Fishing Bridge Junction. The Junction is twenty-seven miles west of the park's closest entrance.

Here it is common to see bison, black and grizzly bears, eagles, otters, and wolves.

By nightfall, all of us felt that we had earned our rest after these morning and evening hikes totaling several miles and the underlying tension of traveling afoot within the domain of the largest land carnivores of the forty-eight states. This was quite a contrast to my roams in the Smokies back home, where the only bears were black and rather passive in comparison to Ol' Griz.

Matt was admirably cautious, and he repeatedly spoke of how we might avoid dangerous encounters regarding mothers with cubs, closeness, surprises (bears do not like surprises!), and food. In addition, we walked in a small pod of two-leggers to form a "bear-proof party" carrying our bear spray.

As time was spent in these open spaces, we began to relax in our demeanor but never in our vigilance. The worst scenario would be to come upon a bear undetected, such as might be the case with a mother tending her cubs or one or more bears intent feeding on carrion or a recent kill.

Later in my GBF association, as Co-President at the Great Bear Foundation 1996 Annual Meeting themed *Bears Around the World,* I would have the honor of presenting a lifetime achievement award to Dr. Barrie Gilbert, honoring him as a giant in the bear world.

In 1977, Gilbert and graduate student Bruce Hastings had been beginning their first week of Yellowstone bear studies when they inadvertently confronted at close range a female grizzly and her cubs. The resulting charge and subsequent injuries that Barrie received required a thousand stitches and left him with permanent facial disfiguration.

Dr. Gilbert, a mild-mannered individual but serious researcher, has dedicated his life's work to the study of bears. Earning a PhD in

Ecology from Duke University, he was once Senior Scientist, Animal Behavior, at Utah State University.

After the horrific 1977 attack, he continued his journey to understand and educate others about bears with an incomprehensible passion for the bruin. Retired now from Utah State, he continues to sport several hats of expertise, like Chuck Jonkel, regarding bear behavior and conservation.

As an offering to our participating members during this annual meeting, GBF scheduled a morning bear viewing trip into Yellowstone. I can well remember the anxiety that I experienced co-leading a sampling of our attendees up Slough Creek in hopes of seeing a bear or two.

As we made our way one behind the other, I noted that more than half of the dozen or so novices conspicuously displayed canisters of pepper spray. It occurred to me that most of them could be a little over zealous for the group's benefit in the usage of this new tool of the trade should we encounter a bear.

I imagined the scene where a bear might suddenly appear a few yards adjacent to the trail we were hiking. The discovery would be blared out, and then I could just envision every can of the fiery eye irritant being emptied into the air about us. No doubt the bear would then delight at the sight of such a gaggle of frail mortals writhing about on the ground, clenching their brows in agony. The affliction and resulting chaos would prove to be harmless and brief, though the recounted humor of it all would no doubt be enjoyed at every fall bear gathering just prior to the extended winter nap.

Thankfully, I was proven wrong and was impressed with the reserve among the group when we actually did encounter a rather blonde-looking grizzly about forty yards away. The bear seemed more intent on investigating a clump of vegetation than in the abundance of eyes that peered at him in astonishment, along with the clicking of numerous camera shutters.

Had I met Barrie Gilbert prior to my first visit to Hayden Valley, I probably would not have ventured one foot beyond the van and would have taken up the cello instead. However, I was in Hayden Valley, this jewel of bear habitat, and our first sighting was just within grasp.

Even from a distance, she was a striking sight, with her long brown hair. There was a silver-tipped halo about her as she strode effortlessly across the horizon with the grace and dignity deserved of such an athletic specimen of a female.

She was *Ursus arctos horriblis*, the grizzly bear. Her cubs-of-the-year appeared just as magnificent yet fearsome as she, these tiny specks did. It was late evening as we scanned them, toward sunset from Trout Creek. For nearly twenty minutes, we were fused to binoculars and spotting scopes as the awesome family unit covered more than two miles before disappearing into the shadows.

Howling wolves from the distant hills put a little spring in my step toward the van a mile away as darkness began to overtake us. Different from hearing the familiar howls in movies or on television, knowing this efficient killing machine was just over the ridge provided considerable motivation to retreat to the vehicle.

Even though we had no wolves in East Tennessee, I knew that there was no data to suggest that wolves consider humans as a food source. Nonetheless, this wisdom somehow paled in comparison to their morose cries and the distance we had to cover before closing the van doors.

On another day in the Hayden, Matt paralyzed us as he looked about where we stood and said, "We should not be here!"

We had proceeded into the valley from the van parked along the roadway about a mile away. Ever alert, we hiked as a small group up and over a number of rolling hills and came into a dusty clearing. Curiosity drew us close to what appeared to be a partially decayed bison.

I was enamored with the spiky horns that protruded from its robust, bushy head. Others innocently investigated various pieces of its scattered remains. It took no time for the excitement of our discovery to slip to fear as Matt immediately coached us away. This was a grizzly kill, a protected stash for future consumption.

Our focus turning from curiosity to observation, we became aware of the immense paw prints that surrounded the carcass, firm with sharp ridges. They were fresh and intimidating.

While casual students of bear encounters might believe that the greatest number of bear attacks occur where there is a both a high concentration of people and bears, this is not the case as borne out by a hundred years of statistics. Most North American bear attacks have occurred in Alaska and Canada, where there are fewer people per square mile of bear habitat than in the Lower Forty-Eight. Yellowstone has had its share of gruesome conflicts.

In examining serious episodes where mauling or death has occurred, stumbling into a stored cache of food or a fresh kill ranks right up there with disturbing a mother bear and her young cubs. Because adult bears will readily defend their prey from neighboring bears or other large mammals, they seldom hesitate to fend off an intruding human.

As Matt barked orders for a rapid retreat, few of us hastened a picture or two of the sizeable prints and rooted up vegetation that obscured the remains from other seekers. One or two would like to have had those shiny black horns that rose from the fallen fortress but time, prudence, and park regulation would not allow it.

As we scurried from the find, I wondered, *Will we walk right up on this bear?* How does one safely retreat from an unseen threat? Regardless, we were rapidly establishing some distance from the carcass and retreating to our van.

In one of our many conversations, Matt had relayed the story of while assisting in bear research, he had admired the enormous head of sedated grizzly while it was cradled in his lap. He told the story over again, how a nearby participant mistakenly dropped a clipboard used to record data collected on the bear. As it clinked onto the ground, the bear immediately awakened and became aware of its surroundings!

The spontaneity of it all left no time to evaluate options. Besides, there was no protocol that promised a suitable outcome. In a state of frigid hysteria, Matt said he never moved, and the animal bolted upward and scampered away from the researchers. Though never mentioned, I suspected that time was spent doing laundry that evening—back where it was safe.

Away from Hayden Valley and the carcass, a visibly shaken Matt led us back to our vehicle, and we sorted out all the possibilities of what could have occurred. None of our assumptions was comforting, though they were exhilarating, since we had made it out unscathed.

Old "Silvertip," likely not too far away from this bruin's prize, chose discretion rather than valor and allowed our unsettled group a pass. We would live another day.

The bison, reduced to a matted rug of hair, strewn bones, and skull, was not so fortunate. Though it saddened me to see such a rugged, impressive animal in this manner, such is the natural cycle of life—without malice, where one animal perishes so that another might live.

Epilogue

Bears need our help, and there are two organizations that I encourage the reader to join and support. They are worthy.

Both are 501(c)(3) non-profit organizations, and therefore financial contributions to them are tax deductable. The operations of both are predominantly carried out by passionate volunteers and a small legend of dedicated staff members.

Each has its own mission, but together their goals make a difference. They accomplish commendable objectives on behalf of bears with minimal funding, through public awareness of bear issues and needs, educational presentations and field trips, efforts in conservation of bear habitat, and direct intervention on behalf of bears in need.

Appalachian Bear Rescue may be found on the Web at www.appalachianbearrescue.org and the address is P.O. Box 364, Townsend, Tennessee 37882.

Its mission is "To rehabilitate orphaned and injured bears for release to the wild; to educate the public about black bears and the regional threats facing them; and to research bear, attributes which may help solve other environmental or health related issues."

Great Bear Foundation may be found on the Web at www. greatbear.org and the address is P.O. Box 9383, Missoula, Montana 59807.

Its mission is "The Great Bear Foundation is a non-profit organization dedicated to the conservation of bears and their habitat around the world."

And finally, *Primum Non Nocere*—
Above All, Do No Harm (to Bears).

Be observant, quiet, and respect their space.
Avoid surprising them and do not get too close.
Properly distance yourself from a mother and her cubs.
Retreat at the first signs of stress in their behavior.
Do not allow your food to become their food.

Enjoy and live with them in harmony!

About the Authors

Joel Zachry has taught outdoor skills courses and led backcountry adventures in black bear and grizzly bear country for over thirty years.

His career as a community college biology professor and naturalist allowed him to combine his occupation with his passion for the outdoors and wildlife. He also served in the mid-1990s as board member and president of Appalachian Bear Rescue and the Great Bear Foundation.

Together with his wife Kathy, a career medical industry executive, he has led extended trips within bear habitat regions of the southern Appalachians, as well as Colorado, Maine, and Montana, and guided excursions in remote portions of Alaska for over twenty years.

Additionally, they section hiked the length of the Appalachian Trail, backpacking 2,175 miles from Georgia to Maine. They completed nearly half of this journey with their beloved dog, "AT," and six loyal hiking friends.

They have served as backcountry instructors, Joel since 1980 and Kathy since 1983, of the nationally recognized, award winning, Smoky Mountain Field School—a cooperative venture between the National Park Service of Great Smoky Mountains National Park and the University of Tennessee.

Retired from their initial careers, they live on seventeen acres in eastern Tennessee with their four cats, fainting goats, and a diversity of wildlife.

They continue to share their knowledge, experiences, and love of the outdoors through their company—Great Outdoors! Adventure Travel.

CPSIA information can be obtained at www.ICGtesting.com
Printed in the USA
LVOW062017300911

248617LV00004B/3/P